BODY
FENG SHUI

BODY
FENG SHUI

The Ancient
Chinese Science
of Body Reading

. . . .

CHAO-HSIU CHEN

Destiny Books
Rochester, Vermont

Destiny Books
One Park Street
Rochester, Vermont 05767
www.InnerTraditions.com

Destiny Books is a division of Inner Traditions International

Library of Congress Cataloging-in-Publication Data

Available at Library of Congress

ISBN 0-89281-769-0

Printed and bound in Canada

10 9 8 7 6 5 4 3 2

Text design and layout by Crystal H. H. Roberts
This book was typeset in Berkeley Book with Omni as the display typeface

Contents

Introduction:
As Outside, So Inside

An old Chinese proverb says, "There is no difference between beauty and luck." From this ancient realization there developed a branch of physiognomy, a branch so profound that it uncovers all aspects of the connection between external appearance and internal character, and gives one insight into what are the proper proportions that constitute harmonious relationships between oneself and others. Because the external is always a mirror of the internal, it is possible to recognize someone's character at a glance, in the lines of the face, the shape of the hands, or the expression in someone's walk. Once we are able to look at our fellow human beings without prejudice in this way, we will be able to avoid unhappiness, hard feelings, or envy because we will automatically choose the right partners.

This knowledge also forms the basis of Feng Shui, the art of placement and of living well that is currently attracting increasing interest in the West. Here, too, the basic assumption is that a harmonic ordering of space can change the character of a place or a person and contribute to happiness, wealth, and good health. Why should what is appropriate for the relation between place and person not also be appropriate for relationships between people? The goal then is to understand the language spoken by the body and thus to avoid the things that are negative, which are mostly man-made, and to appropriate the things that are positive, which are also almost exclusively man-made.

Good Feng Shui rarely exhibits ugliness, but a beautiful person does not necessarily have positive Feng Shui. When you look at your friends and acquaintances you will notice that those who are "beautiful" are not necessarily also successful, while those who are less attractive can be very wealthy. Feng Shui is the ancient Chinese art of placement and system of correspondences that has developed from observing nature for thousands of years. It shows how everything fits together so that heaven and Earth, individual and individual, ego and self, can coexist in harmony. Taoist priests were the ones who applied these discoveries to the human body. They became the founders of the science of physiognomy, which in China is called "Min Xiang Shue"—the teaching of the exploration of fate through the observation of the external appearances of human beings. For the sake of simplicity we call this teaching "Body Feng Shui," where good or bad Body Feng Shui is partly responsible for happiness or unhappiness, success or failure, poverty or wealth, health or illness.

It is important to note at this point that Body Feng Shui is identical with what can be called the "gifts of nature," while one's ultimate fate is always one's own doing. An example will clarify this statement: Even though Barbara Streisand certainly does not have very good Body Feng Shui (for instance, her lips are too big and her nose has an upward slant), she is nonetheless very successful and has always managed her fate positively. And the people that have helped her be successful have found in her a correspondence with their own internal and external picture, which is also the case with regard to the relationship that the singer and actress has to the people with whom she works and has worked. Applying this principle to our own lives, we can check which people have so far corresponded to us, both internally and externally, and which ones have not. We will then find that—externally speaking—it was mostly opposites that attracted (for the internal part it is often that "like attracts"), but the reasons for this are not clear to us. Body Feng Shui shows us *why* we consider some things attractive and others not, and how we may be able consciously (and not instinctively) to find the people that we can get along with, because body language is stronger than we think.

FIGURE 1. Shian Sue Shin Shen, The Internal Reflects the External

1 The Harmony of the Laws

Most people think that they are in control of their own lives. This is only correct in a limited sense (we have the freedom to design our lives *how* we want), as in reality the universe influences our existence at every moment through those laws by which it is governed. Since these laws are in constant interaction with one another, we can safely assume that they accomplish what is often so hard to attain on Earth: harmony. Humanity—apparently because of its special position in nature—is able to disrupt this harmony whenever it likes. For this reason especially it is necessary that humankind seek to realign itself with universal harmony, because otherwise we harm ourselves and our environment. It is thus the most laudable goal for young people to explore and acquaint themselves with the laws of harmony, to abide by them, and be content with them. The most laudable goal in old age, however, is to accept these laws. What takes place in the universe finds its earthly complement in the teachings of Body Feng Shui.

The Energy of the Universe

The human body—like Earth itself—is covered by meridians. These form tracks that enable the energy responsible for our being alive in the first place to move. Because this basic energy cannot be produced solely by ourselves, it must be generated from cooperation with the energy originating from the universe. These meridians (which, as is well known, play a key role

FIGURE 2. Chi, The Energy of The Universe

in acupuncture) constitute what one could call the receiver; the sender is the universe itself, and Earth is the antenna. All living things have such a receiver; they merely have different ways of reacting to the received energies, and, because these energies also influence cellular structures in different ways, this is the reason why people are not only the same, but also different from one another. Thus each person carries his or her own Body Feng Shui as well as his or her own fate.

The Body and the Five Elements

According to the Chinese view, the world is composed of five elements: wood, fire, earth, metal, and water. These are carried by the wind (Feng) and the water (Shui) and are subject to an eternal circulation:

> Wood *feeds* fire,
> fire *turns to ash, which turns to* earth;
> earth *contains* metal;
> metal *foretells* water;
> water *nourishes* wood.

In this cyclical process natural harmony is found in its positive form. There is, however, also a negative complement:

> Wood *fights against* earth;
> earth *against* water;
> water *fights against* fire;
> fire *against* metal;
> metal *against* wood.

This teaching of the five elements is based on the knowledge of *yin* and *yang*, which form the world of complementary opposites. According to this teaching, *yin*, for example, is darkness, earth, moon, woman, stillness, moist, cold, mourning, night, *negative*. *Yang*, on the other hand, symbolizes lightness, sky, sun, man, movement, dry, warmth, happiness, day, *positive*. "Negative" here is not identical with "bad," just as "positive" is not identical with "good." The goal is to find a balance between *yin* and *yang*, between the negative and the positive, so that *harmony* results.

Depending on the time of birth, each person can be assigned one of the five elements. To find out one's element, first one has to know the numerical values of the elements. These are:

Wood	1	2
Fire	3	4
Earth	5	6
Metal	7	8
Water	9	0

To calculate one's number, use the following procedure (which is different for men and women):

Men: Subtract the last two digits of your birth year from the number 100. Divide the result by 9. The result is often a fraction, and only the first numeral *after* the decimal point (the remainder) is of significance. If the result is a whole number, then the number after decimal point is 0.

Example: 100-14=86÷9=9.5; thus one's number is 5, which symbolizes the element *earth*.

Women: Subtract the number 4 from the last two digits of your birth year. Divide the result by 9. Again, only the first numeral after the decimal point is of significance. If the result is a whole number, then the number after the decimal point is 0.

Example: 66-4=62÷9=6.8; thus one's number is 8, which symbolizes the element *metal*.

Here is a general guide to interpreting the different birth elements with regard to personal character (in which—keeping in mind the *yin-yang* nature of human beings—the positive as well as the negative traits are listed):

Wood (1, 2): Good-natured, empathetic, willing to help, honest, open, a loving heart; but also in love with oneself, bears grudges, envious, hypersensitive.

Fire (3, 4): Polite, generous, honest, forward-looking; but also has mood swings, is full of doubts and self-criticism, uncontrolled, without staying power, pedantic, hard.

Earth (5, 6): Faithful, honest, sympathetic, serious, religious, patient, straightforward, correct, trustworthy, conservative, selfless; but also slow, inflexible, in need of comfort, greedy for profit, arrogant, difficult to persuade.

Metal (7, 8): Just, courageous, tolerant, proper, willing to make decisions; but also unfeeling, unhappy, arrogant, unwilling to take another point of view, stubborn.

Water (9, 0): Smart, quick thinker, full of ideas, controlled; but also unheeding, vain, chaotic, and cowardly.

These personality characteristics of the elements form the basis for understanding oneself and other people. But of course these interpretations do not alone suffice, since other factors need to be taken into account in order to get a fuller picture. These include the energy that is contained in each element, which significantly influences the external appearance of the carrier. For these the following traits apply:

Wood (1, 2): Without trees there is no wood. Trees connect Earth with heaven and conduct the cosmic energy of Earth itself. Thus the two main energies of *yin* and *yang* are also connected to one another. Wood passes on this energy to the other elements and to every living thing.

People with the wood element are slim; they rarely walk hunched over; their joints are full of strength; their bones do not protrude through their skin.

Fire (3, 4): Everything that exists can be eaten by fire. Fire, however, cannot ignite itself, nor can it nourish itself.

People with the fire element look dried out and thin; their cheeks are glowing; their bones are visible through their skin.

Earth (5, 6): Earth carries everything living. It gives all things their existence and one day absorbs the energy of living things again.

People with the earth element seem full of strength; their upper arms and thighs are muscular; they have a broad back and a strong behind.

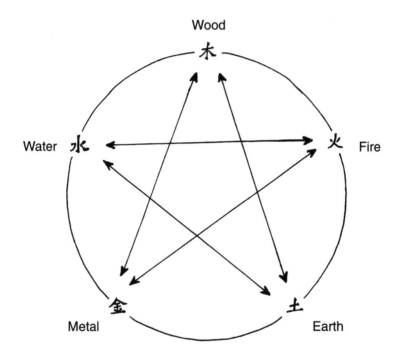

FIGURE 3. The Circle of the Five Elements and
Their Respective Polarities

Metal (7, 8): All metals are hidden somewhere. They are rough, heavy, and shiny.

People with the metal element are often as broad as they are tall; they seem big but not fat; they are big boned.

Water (9, 0): Water represents the perfect circulation system: sea-cloud-rain-river-sea. Water rarely exists in isolation, and usually only in large quantities.

People with the water element are round; their stomachs are usually bloated; their backs are not straight; their bones cannot be touched because of their build.

It should to be noted at this point that the different types of people just described are very rare. Rather, we meet mixtures of types in which two or more elements can be found together. According to the ancient Chinese way of thinking, people that are ruled by only one element, which in turn is identical with the element of their birth, have especially good Body Feng Shui. This means, for example, that a person who is very round and at the same time belongs to the water element can live a very happy life, even if, in a woman, this seems contrary to the prevailing ideal of feminine beauty.

Now that you have figured out which element you or someone you know is ruled by, find out how many positive or negative things pertain to your birth element. If fire is your element and you suffer from self-doubt, you would need a partner who, because of his or her element, is able to balance yours. In this example it would be a water type. If you are polite and honest, however, then a wood type at your side could serve to strengthen these qualities. Having the right partner thus becomes paramount. But what does the "right" partner actually mean?

The Right Partners

All people with whom one is in contact are "partners"—parents, grandparents, teachers, colleagues, friends, business partners, spouses, children. The stronger the relationship is with a person, the more that person is a partner. And the better the elements in the partnership get along, the sooner happiness, health, and success will be realized. The principles of Body Feng Shui show which combinations are suitable or unsuitable. In this case the time of year in which someone was born is also of importance. According to the teaching, the following combinations make for positive outcomes.

Element	Spring	Summer	Fall	Winter
Wood	Water	Water	Metal	Fire
Fire	Wood Fire	Water	Wood Fire	Wood Fire
Earth	Earth Fire	Water	Fire	Fire
Metal	Earth	Earth Water	Earth	Earth
Water	Wood Fire	Metal Water	Metal	Fire

Especially negative outcomes will occur with these combinations:

Element	Spring	Summer	Fall	Winter
Wood	Metal	Fire Metal	Wood	Water
Fire	Water	Wood Fire	Water	Water
Earth	Wood Water	Fire	Water	Water
Metal	Water	Fire	Wood Metal	Wood Metal
Water	Water Earth	Earth	Earth	Earth

Aside from these special combinations, the combination of two elements will have the following effects on a relationship:

Wood-Water combination: Warmth, tenderness, wisdom, acceptance, perseverance, honesty, dynamic thinking, empathy, love of art and success.

Fire-Wood combination: Sensitivity, realistic thinking, prudence, patience, willingness to help, seriousness; but also mistrustfulness and short-term thinking.

Earth-Fire combination: Tenderness, courage, cleverness, need to explore, optimism; but also laziness, absence of modesty, mood swings, indecisiveness.

Metal-Water combination: Largesse of spirit, logical thinking, honesty, tenderness, strength; but also naïveté and risk taking.

Water-Fire combination: Activity, courage; but also self-centeredness, loss of reality, and stress.

Metal-Fire combination: Friendliness, courage; but also stubbornness, egotism, sense of superiority, short-term thinking, ungratefulness.

Metal-Earth combination: Cleverness, honesty, sensitivity, readiness to learn, secrecy, not easily discouraged; but also a need to repeat things and an unwillingness to accept facts.

Earth-Wood combination: Enthusiasm, readiness to make decisions, humane, secrecy, just; but also out of touch with reality, not empathetic

Water-Earth combination: Stability, acceptance; but also unhappiness, self-doubt.

Wood-Metal combination: Creativity, attention to detail, responsibility, generosity, willingness to help; but also impatience, inattention, and fearfulness.

Fire-Fire combination: Courage, fearlessness; but also stress, impatience, heartlessness, disorderliness, and unfriendliness.

Water-Water combination: Straightforwardness, staying power, readiness to accept new ideas, optimism; but also jealousy, mistrustfulness, impatience, and stress.

Wood-Wood combination: Wisdom, empathy, courage, optimism, quest for knowledge, strong sense of justice; but also impatience, mistrustfulness, stubbornness, impulsiveness, feeling of superiority, narrow-mindedness.

Earth-Earth combination: Obedience, seriousness, carefulness, generosity, optimism; but also stubbornness, impatience, eccentricity, indecision.

Metal-Metal combination: Ambition, courage, politeness; but also impatience and lack of forgiveness.

If you have or have had difficulties or problems with one of your "partners," then now, using the element combinations, you will recognize why. Of course the same also goes for positive aspects. But if two elements simply do not work together, it may be better to look for a new, more suitable partner rather than waste energy on the wrong element. But please reflect carefully before you separate yourself from an unsuitable element. At times it also makes sense to choose the lesser of two evils. If it is not possible for you to enter a new element combination, then insist on strengthening the positive aspects of the present combination and on ignoring the negative ones.

The Five Elements and Health

Each life is different, yet all lives follow the same cycle of being born, growing old, getting sick, dying. Nobody can escape this cycle, no more than one can escape the changing of the seasons. That is why it is important to adjust to this rhythm in order to live long and well and without too many disturbances. The five-element theory forms the right starting point for making this adjustment. It played a very important role in healing and medicine in ancient China because of its influence on the five most important organs (heart, lungs, liver,

相伴兩不厭

FIGURE 4. Shian Ban Lian Bu Yen, To Be Happy Together in One

kidneys, spleen). The following correspondences are of particular interest in the study of the Body Feng Shui:

wood-liver-eyes

fire-heart-tongue

earth-spleen-skin

metal-lungs-nose

water-kidneys-ears

An example will clarify these correspondences. Person M has a very fine sense of smell, but very bad eyes. On the one hand, this means that person M has very good lungs, but also a somewhat problematic (this does not mean sick!) liver. According to the five-element teaching this means that in their expression metal is very strong and wood very weak. The lack of wood causes a further disadvantage: there is not enough fire to keep the heart "burning." Person M in this respect thus has to anticipate problems in this area—sooner or later. To deal with this problem, the five-element teaching suggests that person M should be with someone who has a very strong wood element to balance the problem. Furthermore, a diet with more of the wood element can also help to balance the situation. This diet would consist mainly of "green" or "red" foods, as illustrated in the following table.

Wood	green	zucchini, spinach, green peppers, beans, peas, kiwi, etc.
Fire	red	meat, red peppers, red apples, radishes, tomatoes, etc.
Earth	yellow	bananas, lemons, pumpkin, egg yolks, corn, etc.
Metal	white	fish, potatoes, noodles, rice, bread, chicken, etc.
Water	black	black beans, seaweed, morels, etc.

Figure 5. I Chien, The First Look

Different tastes have also been assigned to the different elements. These are:

Wood	sour	liver	eyes
Fire	bitter	heart	tongue
Earth	sweet	spleen	skin
Metal	spicy	lungs	nose
Water	salty	kidneys	ears

To cure illnesses of the most important internal organs as well as of the senses, one has to pay attention to the rhythm of the five elements and their respective polarities (as shown in figure 3 on page 10). For example, someone who has liver problems should eat spicy foods, since liver belongs to wood, and is controlled by metal, which is spicy in nature. A different example: Someone who has heart troubles should eat very salty foods, since heart belongs to fire, and fire is controlled by water, which has a salty character.

In Body Feng Shui such consideration of the five elements is of great significance, because ultimately the goal is to recognize appropriate partners and lead a happy life. The latter is hardly possible without good health, and for the former it is important to grasp at a glance in what physical condition one's potential partner is in—because in the end one will sooner or later form a team (either professional or personal in nature) with that person. If one chooses the wrong partner, sooner or later this will damage one's own health and have a negative influence on one's progress. To recognize whether a person will influence one positively or negatively, a look at their hair will suffice:

1, 2	wood	liver	eyes	eyebrows, eyelashes
3, 4	fire	heart	tongue	hair on head
5, 6	earth	spleen	skin	hair on arms, legs, and chest

| 7, 8 | metal | lungs | nose | nose hair |
| 9, 0 | water | kidneys | ears | facial and underarm hair, pubic hair |

An example will clarify this: You meet person N and want to know whether he is a suitable partner. His arm-hair growth is extremely strong, which means he exhibits an excess of the earth element. Such a person will have taut skin. To find out whether person N is suitable for you, calculate your own element (as explained previously) and check whether it works with the earth element of person N (as shown in figure 3 on page 10). The "recognition" of a person is thus to a high degree dependent upon external appearance, and there is more truth in this appearance than is commonly believed. Body Feng Shui teaches us to recognize this truth at first glance, in order to avoid later disappointments.

Blood Types and Personality

As mentioned earlier, Body Feng Shui is first of all the teaching of the proper selection of partners. Because these—especially in the case of love—have effects on following generations, modern Body Feng Shui also teaches what personality types can be ascribed to the different blood types. The following correspondences become clear:

Type A: Melancholic, reserved, mistrustful, shy, secretive, un-diplomatic, a loner, sentimental; but also bighearted, faithful, sensible, thoughtful, artistic, tender, empathetic, serious, imaginative, patient.

Type B: Vain, boasting, talkative, direct, curious, impatient, mood swings; but also diplomatic, logical, athletic, well spoken, active, not sentimental, flexible, enjoys life.

Type AB: Melancholic, shy, unsteady, doubtful, cheap, self-centered, talkative, a loner, vain, impatient, full of contradictions; but also tender, bighearted, logical, sensible, serious, reserved, diplomatic, athletic, flexible.

Figure 6. Chung Tse, A Noble Person

Type O: Arrogant, unbending, greedy, disobedient, insisting; but also patient, logical, unemotional, generous, self-sufficient, diplomatic, modest, imaginative, courageous, decisive, thoughtful.

By using the knowledge about the character of the blood types on the basis of the five-element teaching, one can avoid mistakes in the choice of partners from the start. At the same time, this knowledge about the personality traits of a possible partner also offers the opportunity to think about whether oneself or a partner is really active in the truly right field. The following jobs (only a sample) are thus accorded to the various blood types, where exceptions of course prove the rule:

Type A: teacher, nurse, priest, monk, nun, ranger, fisherman, librarian, administrator.

Type B: diplomat, businessman, artist, scientist, computer programmer, doctor, athlete, architect.

Type AB: veterinarian, mailman, architect, all religious positions and callings, psychologist, psychiatrist, psychotherapist, health practitioner.

Type O: soldier, athlete, banker, financial consultant, secret agent, manager, politician.

But because each job is performed by a person who has his or her own character, this aspect too has to be considered in the choice of partners (both professional and private), as is shown in the next chapter.

FIGURE 7. Tsen, A Good Nature

Habits and Character

We have all heard the saying, "You reap what you sow." In China, this proverb is more elaborate:

> *When you plant a deed,*
> *you harvest a habit;*
> *when you plant a habit,*
> *you harvest a character;*
> *when you plant a character,*
> *you harvest fate;*
> *when you plant fate,*
> *you harvest a life.*

Everybody has habits, be they wanted or not. All habits are closely related to the psyche and offer clues to a person's character. A sensitive person can tell the whole character of another person by the smallest habit.

Habits form over the years, without a person's noticing. Habits derive mostly from wishes that cannot or are not allowed to find their expression and are thus transported to other parts of the body. For example, people that are very angry will clench and grind their teeth, even though anger and teeth are not directly related. Apparently, in this case, a psychological process is elevated to a physical level in order, on the one hand, to alleviate the soul, and on the other, to express the situation. A different example: If somebody is suddenly happy because of a surprising event, he will often jump with joy, shaking arms and legs, "dancing with joy." Here too the psyche finds a physical expression.

All of these forms of bodily expression occur repeatedly in the same manner, as the soul itself and the body have been conditioned to act in this way. These always similar expressions have the benefit that other people can quickly tell what mood another is in, and thus react accordingly.

義

FIGURE 8. I, Courage

Here are some examples of certain types of behavior and their causes:

Biting the nails: One is not happy with an external situation (or a person), but does not have the strength to change the situation (or the person), or to leave it. This will lead to excessive obedience, self-esteem problems, a lack of concentration, and impatience.

Rubbing the chin: One is caught up in a difficult situation, and there is nobody with whom one can talk it through in confidence. This will lead to a lack of courage and mood swings.

Sagging shoulders and head: One is confronted with a problem for which there seems to be no solution. No matter what is done, it will simply make matters worse. This will lead to extreme reservation, shyness, melancholy, and pessimism.

Tapping the feet: One does not agree with the opinion of a partner, but does not dare to express it. This results in impatience and envy.

Tapping the fingers: One is annoyed because projected goals are not met or because expected people are not arriving. This leads to coldness and mistrustfulness.

Touching the nose: One is dissatisfied because things are not starting out as desired. Furthermore, one has too many wishes for all of them to be fulfilled. This results in a correct self-assessment, courage, and stress.

Biting the lower teeth on the upper lip: One is developing new ideas or is searching for new ways to reach a goal. This results in a willingness to take risks and aggressiveness.

FIGURE 9. Li, Awe

Rubbing the hands: One is happy because something was accomplished without a larger confrontation. This results in honesty, seriousness, and conflict-avoiding strategies.

Finger games: One concentrates only on one's own affairs and does not listen to what others are saying. This leads to nervousness, ignorance, arrogance, and self-centeredness.

Constant laughter: One is insecure because of a person or a situation. This leads to impatience, insecurity, self-centeredness, and the desire for more attention.

Based on the knowledge of such behavioral patterns, their psychological causes, and their psychological effects, the five-element teaching can establish correlations among the five elements, which in turn are congruent with five of the character traits lauded by Confucius (figures 7 to 11). This allows for a proper partner selection based on body language, which in turn can lead to a happy life. These relationships can be described as follows:

Wood	goodness
Fire	awe
Earth	faith
Metal	courage
Water	wisdom

According to the Chinese view, the person who, after having found his element, lets the corresponding characteristic become his habit is most laudable. Of course everybody is free to incorporate *all five* characteristics in his personality.

The Chi in Human Beings

When we speak of Body Feng Shui, we also have to think about what it is that enables a body to live. Some readers may say, of course, that

FIGURE 10. Tsche, Wisdom

it is the heart and the working of the other organs. That is correct, but what sustains those organs? In the Chinese system it is *chi*, the omnipotent force of life, that makes life possible. Among Indians this force is called *prana*, the ancient Greeks called it *pneuma*, the Japanese *ki*, the Polynesians *nana*, and the Germans *odem*. Nobody can live without *chi*. This universal energy gives us the strength to lead a life of harmony and to grow into a mature, happy, and beautiful personality. That is exactly what *chi* does, which is why special attention is paid to it in Feng Shui teaching and especially in the study of Body Feng Shui. *Chi*, as the Chinese know, is even visible—in the different color nuances of the skin, where color does not refer to the skin color of one's race, but rather what "shines" through the skin, the mysterious energy of life. For Feng Shui experts it is easy to tell what physical and psychological condition a person is in and under what conditions he is presently living from a glance at the color in his face. The significance of *chi* for health and happiness goes so far that in China one not only asks, "How are you?" but can also say instead, "Your *chi* color looks especially good today!"

The *chi* colors are as follows: green/blue; burgundy; red/purple; yellow; white; and black. The meaning of these colors is as follows:

Green/blue: One is suffering a little, but the reason for this is not fundamental.

Burgundy: The five elements in the body, which are assigned to the various organs, are not in their productive order; especially fire and water are not in harmony.

Red/purple: Something positive will occur.

Yellow: The five elements in the body are not in harmony, especially wood and earth, meaning liver and spleen.

White: Something causing mourning will occur.

Black: Something negative will occur, but if the black is especially "glowing," the opposite, meaning something positive, will occur.

FIGURE 11. Schin, Loyalty

This already shows how incredibly complex a subject the "*chi* color" is, especially when one considers that this type of observation also depends on the season and the time of day, as well as the body area where the color is "measured." There is thus truly the need for an expert, and it is wrong to leave the interpretation of the colors to a lay person.

Nonetheless, here is a small peek into the "relations":

1, 2	wood	green (blue)
3, 4	fire	red (purple/burgundy)
5, 6	earth	yellow
7, 8	metal	white
9, 0	water	black

How these correspondences work together with the months is shown in the following table.

MONTH	COLOR	POSITIVE (0) NEGATIVE (X)
January, February (wood)	green	0
	red	0
	yellow	X
	white	X
	black	0
April, May (fire)	green	X
	red	X
	yellow	0
	white	X
	black	0

July, August (metal)	green	X
	red	0
	yellow	0
	white	0
	black	0
October, November (water)	green	0
	red	0
	yellow	X
	white	X
	black	X
March, June, September, December (earth)	green	X
	red	0
	yellow	0
	white	X
	black	X

Some readers will be surprised that none of these secrets are known in the West. We do not want to speculate on the reasons for this, but hope that this will change thoroughly with the publication of this book. The harmony of the laws is the same everywhere, be it in China, America, or Europe. This of course also applies to the laws of harmony and attraction, which are presented in the next chapter.

FIGURE 12. Chi-Se, Chi Color

2 The Laws of Harmony

In the Body Feng Shui teaching of ancient China, the face is divided into three parts. The first part (the forehead to the eyebrows) reflects the sky, the second part (from the eyebrows to the tip of the nose) embodies the person himself, and the third part (from the tip of the nose to the chin) represents Earth.

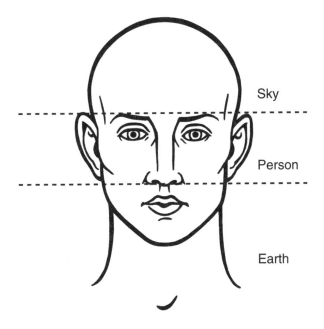

FIGURE 13. The Three Parts of Harmony

Because of the ideal according to which sky, person, and Earth are supposed to be in perfect harmony, this concept also applies to the proportional division of the face. But all laws that can be found in nature, in the sky, even in the universe, are not separate from human beings. On the contrary, because each denizen of Earth is a living part of the whole, she also carries in herself those laws that make up the whole. It is understandable that these laws are subject to harmony (even chaos theory has discovered that there is nothing purely chaotic, but that chaos too is shaped by harmony—even if this harmony is not always visible). Not only do the laws themselves partake of this harmony but also everything that is subject to these laws. The part and the whole are thus not only in relation to one another, but also indivisibly connected. If one part is no longer "correct," the harmony is disturbed. And if the natural harmony is disturbed, it is necessary to learn to rectify this disturbance so that a new harmony can be formed. That is why a Chinese proverb says, "Recognize the laws of nature, take them as they are, and find happiness." This applies in particular to the first body part that we shall now discuss, the eyes.

FIGURE 14. Yuen Man, The Round Fullness

The Eyes: "Crystals in the Morning Dew"

About 1,800 years ago in China there lived a famous princess, who was abducted during a war. Because of her extraordinary beauty she was not killed but was instead chosen as the main wife of the chief of the rebel party. As the "goddess of the Lo River" she even found her entrance into literature. She was described as not needing to open her lips, since for anything she wanted to say a glance from her eyes would suffice. In Chinese culture the eyes are also called the "window to the soul." They are believed to be the most important of the sense organs.

Generally speaking, the distance between the pupil and the eyebrow should be neither too big nor too small. If the iris and the white part of the eye are clearly separated from one another, this bears testimony to positive eye Feng Shui, as does an iris that is marked by its glowing shine. Eyes are supposed to give an active impression, and the "personality" that can then be found in the eyes adds additional emphasis to them.

Many different shapes of eyes exist, each of them having a special significance. What follows is an explanation of the twenty-three most important shapes.

1   2

1. The triangular shape indicates that the bearer has a lot of courage. If the iris and the white part of the eye are separated from one another this means that there is a tendency to go to extremes, yet without doing harm to others. If the iris and the white part are not clearly separated, however, this means that one will be successful, but that the means used will not always be honorable. For women with the latter type this means that they have troubles concentrating and often cause problems for others.

2. Here the low-lying iris is surrounded by white on three sides. People with this type of eyes are often very hard and speak ill of others. They do not suffer from self-esteem problems, even when they are not especially intelligent.

3   4

3. Here the high-lying iris is surrounded by white on three sides. The owners of such eyes are often indifferent toward others. For men this shape means that they always occupy themselves, even with dangerous things. For women this shape means that there are frequently problems with partners.

4. The iris is entirely surrounded by white. Such eyes speak of a disregard for others, a bad temper, and an insatiable sexual appetite.

5   6

5. Black spot in the white of the eye: an unsteady character. Family property is not in good hands with this person.

6. The iris is full of differently colored spots: not very friendly, but also not bad enough to harm others; big difficulties in the attainment of goals.

7   8

7. In the iris small lines of a different color occur (similar to those in chickens): bad characteristics are in the majority; very rough and unfriendly.

8. The iris resembles the ring of fire found in a circus: tells of impatience and a very weak character; friendships are rare.

9   10

9. The entire inside of the eyes is very unclear, much like with a drunk person. The laughing wrinkles point downward and the pupil is not in the center. The shape of the eyes, including the wrinkles, is reminiscent of a fish. People with such eyes are not very picky—including in the sexual realm.

10. Reminiscent of bow and arrow. The pupil points upward, and the iris and white of the eye are without clear separation. This eye seems always to be smiling. With such eyes one is assured the sympathy of the opposite sex. Insatiable not only in the sexual realm; very smart and clever.

11. Reminiscent of a fish without a tail. The pointed end points toward the nose, the blunt end to the ear. Such people try their hardest to impress the opposite sex. They often use their talent unwisely.

They do not always stick to the truth to attain their goals, which can bring them into uncomfortable situations.

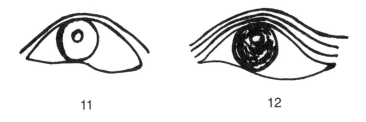

11   12

12. Reminiscent of the eye of a lion: very big and demanding of respect. Colored and white parts are sharply separated. The iris is a little above the middle, the eyelid shows three or more "rolls." Such eyes stand for a noble character, friendliness, tenderness, and a largesse of spirit. People with such eyes (rare among women) and with a lot of power will never abuse their power.

13   14

13. Reminiscent of the eye of a tiger: large shape with a golden shine of colors, and the laughing wrinkles point upward. This eye looks straight ahead with a good deal of force. The owners of such eyes (rare among women) are courageous, intelligent, honest, stand their ground, and are well equipped for wealth.

14. Reminiscent of the eye of a monkey. The shape is round and there is a yellow shine in the pupil. Pupil, iris, and eyelid seem to be pointed upward. People with such eyes usually keep their head bent and blink frequently. They have an active, courageous, and very creative character. They are always in action and never rest. While they do not help anybody, they also do not cause any harm.

15   16

15. Reminiscent of the eye of an elephant: very narrow and long with three or more lid rolls. The expression is friendly and good, and so is the character. Great wisdom is found here.

16. Reminiscent of the eye of a bird: very narrow and long, with the iris located in the upper part. The glow is yellow and the lid has only one fold. The character is very unbalanced; such people have troubles getting along with others and therefore often tend to remain alone.

17   18

17. Reminiscent of the eye of a bird of prey. The pupil is mostly dark with a golden shine. The eye is surrounded by a lid on top and bottom, and the expression is very clear. Such eyes tell of friendliness and harmony; their owners can accumulate great wealth.

18. Reminiscent of the eye of a swallow. It is deep in the socket and very long. The colored and white parts are clearly separated from one another and are surrounded by a thick lid on top and bottom. The expression is glowing. People with such eyes have a very pure character; they keep their promises and can be trusted.

19. Reminiscent of the eye of a stork: it is large and round and from the top is bordered by several lid rolls. The colored and white

parts are clearly separated from one another. If one looks into such an eye, one experiences spiritual strength and the strength to stand one's ground. People with such eyes are straightforward, generous, open-minded, and generally well liked.

19   20

20. Reminiscent of the eye of a cow: it is large and round. The colored part is round too and clearly separated from the white. Such eyes look very mildly and are bordered by a roll on the top and bottom; the laughing wrinkles point upward. People with such eyes are very willing to help, loving, and well liked.

21   22

21. Reminiscent of the eye of a horse. The skin that holds it is fairly loose and has several rolls below it, but only one on the top. The laughing wrinkles are slanted slightly upward. This eye seems to be constantly tearing. People with such eyes have to work hard, but often their labors do not bring them any success; they also have troubles with relationships.

22. Reminiscent of the eye of a sheep, with no rolls on the top or bottom. The laughing wrinkles are slanted upward. The colored part is often freckled, causing a slightly cloudy appearance. The owners of such eyes have to work hard in life; for them nothing comes easy. Even if they have a family estate it will bring worries to them.

23

23. Reminiscent of the eye of a pig. It is surrounded by heavy, thick skin, it stares blankly, and it has a slightly outward curve. It shows no external line and the white part has a cloudy appearance. People with such eyes are very unfriendly and have no scruples; they also often exhibit criminal energies.

FIGURE 15. Inn Inn, Crystals in the Morning Dew

The Nose: "The Mountain of the Tender Dragon"

Before we turn to the significance of the nose in Body Feng Shui, it is necessary to mention six important points.

In the teaching of Body Feng Shui the nose is considered the key to the understanding of the relation between a person and wealth as well as the relation between personality and romantic happiness.

Generally speaking, parts A through C should form a straight line, parts D and E should be of the same type, and part F should not be too high (upward slanting) and not too pointy. Just as among eyes, there are different types of noses, each of which has a particular significance. What follows are the twelve most common types.

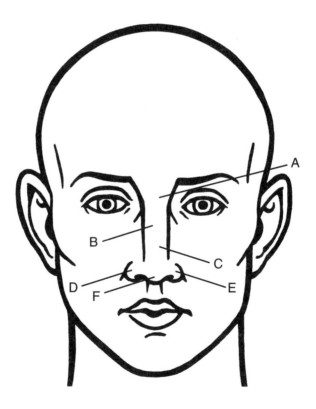

FIGURE 16. The Important Points of the Nose

1. Part *A* is broad and thick, clearly pronounced. Parts *B* and *C* are straight and full, *D* and *E* are similar, and *F* is fleshy. Such a nose tells of large, lifelong wealth. People with such a nose are honest, just, and fair. This is the fame and wealth nose.

2. *A* is flat, *B* and *C* are connected by a round arc, *D* and *E* have a clear character, and *F* is full and fleshy. The bearer of such a nose may be wealthy and well regarded and is very intelligent, worldly-wise, and just. This is the nose of a Mongolian sheep.

3. *A*, *B*, and *C* are on the same beautiful line, but not too high. *D* and *E* are similar to one another and not too large, *F* is full. Such a nose tells of happiness, a long life, wealth, harmony, and unpretentiousness. It is Bambi's nose.

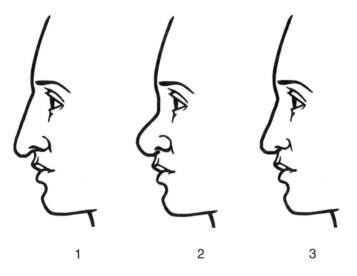

| 1 | 2 | 3 |

4. *A*, *B*, and *C* are on an extreme and sharp line, without flesh. *F* is pointed and without flesh. People with such a nose have a correct character, work hard throughout their lives, and are not particularly lucky in the personal realm. This nose is reminiscent of a sword.

5. This nose looks as though *A* is below *B* and *C*. *F*, however, is pointed upward, which is why *A* only appears to be below *B* and *C*. The entire nose seems to be very big, even if it is not very fleshy. Such a nose tells of intelligence, a kind heart, a willingness

to learn; the relationship to relatives is not very good. This nose could be described as the "Matterhorn."

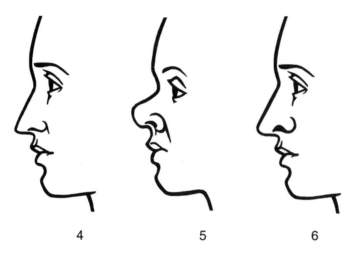

6. Upon looking at this nose, the large openings of *D* and *E* are noticeable. *A*, *B*, and *C*, however, make for a nicely slanted line, and *F* is not fleshy. This nose tells of courage, a sense of justice, and ambition. It is reminiscent of two open fans.

7. *B* and *C* here form a hump. The entire nose is large, but not very fleshy. People with such a nose have trouble getting along with others, and mostly stay by themselves. They often react strangely and are self-centered, yet they are honest. It is the nose of a camel.

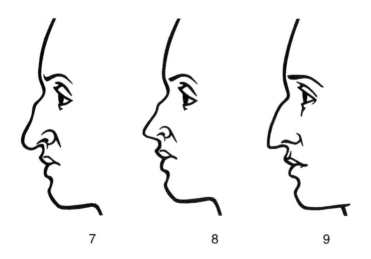

8. *A* lies in a cave, *B* resembles a hill, and *C* again lies in a cave. *F* sticks out sharply. The bearer of such a nose has mood swings and is strange; problems with the opposite sex are bound to occur. This nose reminds one of an **S** with three turns.

9. *B* and *C* lie high, but are slanted. *F* is long and sharp. People with such a nose are often aggressive, take risks, and are full of dark plans. This nose reminds one of an eagle.

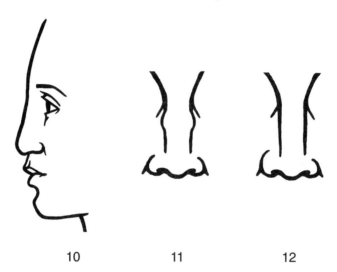

10   11   12

10. The nose and forehead form a line that almost touches the face. Such a nose indicates a weak character; its bearer often makes mistakes, but is always guided by good intentions. While the nose ridge and forehead also form a line in a classical Greek nose, this line does not touch the face. The character of a Greek nose is the opposite of this one.

11. The peculiarity of this nose is easier to spot from the front. *B* and *C* form a hump that stretches to the left and to the right. People with such a nose are very mean and stubborn and tend to go to extremes. This nose resembles a knot.

12. This nose has a very beautiful line, but *D* and *E* are not of the same kind. People with such a nose have to work hard throughout their entire lives and are not very astute in financial affairs. This nose is so extraordinary that no comparison should be made.

FIGURE 17. Wuo Long Shan, The Mountain of the Tender Dragon

The Lips: "The Shores of the Murmuring Creek"

In ancient China there was a great artist who was an excellent composer, dancer, and singer, as well as a remarkable poet. For a performance before the emperor he recited the following poem:

In our country there lives a girl
who is lovely, tender, and of great beauty.
But she lives in isolation, nobody can see her.
If she lived among people and would smile only once,
the entire city would be at her feet.
And if she smiled a second time,
the entire country would kneel down before her.

The very excited emperor asked his advisor: "Does this girl really exist, or is she only a fantasy of our poet?" The advisor excitedly whispered: "Oh, yes, my emperor, she exists; she is even the sister of our poet, who wrote this poem just for her." The end of the story is predictable: The emperor met the girl and fell in love. Soon after the entire country knelt down before the smile of two wonderful lips.

To understand Asia one needs to know that there the smile is regarded more highly than laughter. It is for this reason that Japan is called "the country of smiles," and in China a saying goes, "If you say 'yes,' smile. If you say 'no,' smile! If you are silent, smile!"

Regardless what type of smile it is, it always appears on the lips. In Body Feng Shui, the following apply to the lips: they should exhibit a clear shape, not be too thin, but also not too big, and should always be full of color. When one smiles, the teeth should not be visible.

In the following diagrams the ten most important lip shapes are pictured.

1   2

1. This shape means honesty, intelligence, and seriousness. It leads to success, wealth, long life, health, and possibly many children.

2. Here you can recognize a soft and tender character of the highest intelligence. A person with such lips is very well liked, successful, and wealthy.

3   4

3. This shape speaks of intelligence. The owner of such lips can speak well, is successful in her career, and is thus quite wealthy.

4. Someone with such lips is certainly not a happy person. These people are up to no good, always speak ill of others, and usually tend to stay alone throughout their lives.

5   6

5. These lips tell of a lonely character who is unfriendly and has had to suffer all her life. Only rarely will such a person experience even minor success.

6. A person with these lips is unable to keep any secret and is also a strong critic. She often makes the wrong calculations and is unable to keep a family estate.

7   8

7. Never trust these lips. They offer false compliments; their owners are unable to keep up a relationship and only rarely have any friends.

8. People with such lips like to speak ill of others, turn their partners' words around, and have no sense of justice.

9   10

9. People with such lips and teeth are not able to guard money; they lead a very unsteady life, frequently change their place of residence, and like to take risks.

10. These lips speak of a very unsteady character. People with such lips and teeth should beware of accidents as well as financial losses.

In addition, the following points can be made:

- People whose lips are full and well colored and whose lip corners point upward are generally of a friendly and happy nature.

- Full lips are always better than thin ones, but only when they go along with the other facial proportions.

- People who continually press their lips together are not very honest.

- A pout usually tells of an insatiable appetite—in every realm.

- If the mouth is large and out of proportion to the rest of the face, the person often makes unfulfilled plans and cannot manage her time.

- People who rarely open their lips are very straightforward and serious thinkers.

- If the upper lip protrudes past the lower lip, this indicates a self-esteem problem. Such people often make wrong plans and cause a lot of damage.

- For men: If the upper lip is bigger than the lower lip, this tells of a steady character.

- For women: If the lower lip is bigger than the upper lip, this tells of patience and tenderness.

FIGURE 18. Ho Pan Tsong Tsong, The Shores of the Murmuring Creek

The Teeth: "Lotus Flowers in the Mud"

Teeth should be straight and strong, and mostly close together. Furthermore, white and shiny teeth are advantageous even if they are not short and straight. The gums should be mostly out of sight. In China it is said that women whose gums become visible when they open their mouths are very loose in love affairs. Men whose gums are visible are said to be less concerned about morals.

People who have small open spaces between their teeth are said to be bad with money.

Each person has twenty-eight to thirty-two teeth. The more teeth a person has, the more active his heart, his soul, and his mind will be; that is why one should carefully think about having a tooth pulled—teeth are the jewelry of the mouth. They resemble lotus flowers, whose petals please the observer through their beauty.

出汙泥而不染

FIGURE 19. Tsou Wu Ni Er Bu Zan, Lotus Flowers in the Mud

The Eyebrows: "Snakes in the Garden of the Temple"

The philosopher Dschiang Tse once said: "The most minor of things can also be the most important of things." With regard to eyebrows, this sage seems to be right, as one might think that eyebrows are completely useless in the face when one compares them to the significance of the nose, eyes, mouth, and ears. This, however, is not true. Without eyebrows we would not be able to see as well, because they keep the sweat of the forehead from running into our eyes. Furthermore, the face without eyebrows would not be very attractive.

Generally speaking the following points apply to eyebrows in the teaching of Body Feng Shui:

- It is good if the hairs are soft and firm at the same time.

- It is also good if they grow in the same direction.

- The darker the color, the better.

- The starting point of a brow should be the same as the starting point of an eye.

- The end of the brow should be a little bit behind the end of the eye, toward the ear.

- If an eyebrow in the direction of the ear is a little (the emphasis being "a little") too short or too long, then it is not bad enough to cause any damage.

- If an eyebrow is too long toward the nose, however, it is not only not attractive, but also telling of a very short-tempered person.

- If an eyebrow is too short toward the nose, this speaks of a lack of courage and opinions.

- The eyebrows should be full, but it is good if every single hair is visible when regarded more closely.

- A thick eyebrow generally speaks of courage.

- A thin eyebrow suggests less courage, but a thorough nature.

- If the hairs at the beginning of the eyebrow grow irregularly in different directions, this means that their bearer likes taking risks and is not willing to engage in a discussion.

- If the hairs grow irregularly at the end of the brow, this means that their bearer is narrow-minded and not very trustful and has mood swings. Furthermore, he is dishonest and not eager to learn.

- For people with birthmarks on their eyebrows the following applies: If the mark is black or red or very shiny, this means that the bearer is unusually intelligent and furthermore a very noble character. If the color of the mark is unclear or not shiny this does not meaning anything good or bad.

In order to be able to form a better picture of the different types of eyebrows, the fifteen most important shapes are explained here.

1   2   3

1. "The long-living star." Long, broad shape; each hair is very long and grows downward. This shape stands for a long and healthy life. People with such brows are very friendly and multitalented and are sexually very active.

2. "The sleeping tiger." The bearer of these eyebrows usually looks angry, but in reality is very friendly. Such a person is interested in spiritual as well as in material matters and is extremely ambitious.

3. "The sleeping silk-cocoon." Such eyebrows are supposed to lead to wealth, fame, and a long life. The bearer is very often smart and eager to learn, straightforward, and trusting. He or she is equally interested in spiritual and material matters.

| 4 | 5 | 6 |

4. "Eyebrow of pureness." It guarantees a comfortable life free of worries. People with such brows are family types, make good friends, and never disappoint.

5. "The dragon." In ancient China it was said that people with such brows should be respected like an emperor. Such people are very smart, have outstanding personalities, are courageous, and have a steady character.

6. "The machete." These brows are not as dangerous as their name suggests, and can lead their bearer to success even at the beginning of life. Such bearers have a tough personality; they do not accept advice or counsel, but are very courageous, and always want to be victorious. They often hurt others without meaning to do so.

| 7 | 8 | 9 |

7. "The willow leaf." People with such brows can be successful, and even if they are not famous, they are usually at least wealthy. People with this type of eyebrow are very mild and have good personalities. They are smart and eager to learn; at the same time they are also honest and faithful.

8. "The half-moon." People with these brows can be very successful in their career, and can pass this success on to their family and relatives. They are sensible, have a pure heart full of love, are friendly and loving, and are unusually willing to help.

9. "The scissors." Mostly very short brows. People that have to live with these eyebrows are probably not going to be very successful in any of their endeavors. They are not very astute in their thinking and their actions, do not respect property, and can only survive by dishonorable means. Happily enough, this shape is very rare among women.

| 10 | 11 | 12 |

10. "The sword." People with such brows often have a very varied life. They therefore also have to exert themselves more in order to be successful. Such people can look impatient or harmless, but they rarely do good deeds. They have a very strong temper.

11. "The broom." Brows of this type speak of success until midlife, after which this success will be hard to maintain. People that have these brows are not very sentimental or loving, but they keep their promises.

12. "The windsock." People with such brows either are not successful but lead a quiet life, or are successful but without any positive effects. These people look very noble, but in reality are quite the opposite and always pretend as if they are especially trustworthy and lovable. They cannot get enough of money and sex.

13   14   15

13. "The mongoose bean." Bearers of such eyebrows often have to work very hard to survive. They usually prefer to stay by themselves. They have a bad temper and are unfeeling, dishonest, and greedy.

14. "The spiral." These brows can lead to success if the other characteristics of Body Feng Shui are good as well. If this is not the case, they will have a difficult life. But they are generally full of courage and very motivated; however, they do not have a love of family.

15. "The straight." If the other Body Feng Shui characteristics are positive, then people with these eyebrows can be very successful, even early in life. But if the other Body Feng Shui characteristics are negative, such people will lead very ordinary lives in which only rarely will something especially positive take place.

FIGURE 20. She Yuen Long Inn, Snakes in the Garden of the Temple

The Ears: "Leaves on the Tree of Hope"

Aside from their hearing function, little attention is usually paid to ears. This is in spite of the fact that in addition to the regions important for acupuncture, there are also regions on the ears that are very important for amorous encounters. Generally speaking, the following characteristics should be paid attention to:

- The ear should be "well defined," meaning that it is good if the individual details are all equally clear.

- The length of the ear is important. At the top it should end at the height of the end of the eyebrow, at the bottom at the level of the tip of the nose.

- The ear should be close to the head.

- The earlobe should be large, thick, and soft.

- Earlobes that are attached to the head are less desirable.

- Even though they say "the bigger, the better," the ear should nonetheless be in proportion to the face.

- If the ear is proportionally too large, one's luck will not be negatively influenced; however, the personality of people with such ears is at times a little strange.

- If the ear is proportionally too small, one's luck can resemble a sine curve. Such people have little courage and little staying power.

- If the ear extends too far past the eyebrow, such people will not have much luck in life. On the other hand, they often develop extraordinary talents and have much knowledge in a particular area. They are furthermore very emotional, but also like to show off with their own talents.

- If the ear ends far below the eyebrow, this means that such people rarely have any special knowledge, but are better at organizing their daily lives. They like order and a comfortable life.

- If the ear is proportionally very small, the person lacks intelligence.

- If the ear forms a sharp tip at the top, the bearer, while not without feelings, is not loving and can cause harm.

- If the ear is proportionally very large, well shaped, and lighter than the face, this speaks of great fame or wealth or possibly both.

- If the color of the ear is dark red or looks burned, no great wealth should be expected, and the health will not be the best.

- The thicker and more consistent an ear feels, the better the bearer is with regard to financial matters.

- If an ear feels especially thin, this can be a sign of a problem in dealing with money, other people, or the person's own health.

- If the ears are of different sizes, it can be assumed that the bearer is clumsy.

- The same applies if the ears do not run in a straight line to the neck.

Figure 21. Wen, Perceiving

FIGURE 22. Tschue Wu, Understanding

In Body Feng Shui the ears (much like in acupuncture) play a special role, which is why it is necessary to point out the most important regions (see A–G in figure 23) that we shall now consider in relation to the five-element teaching. Doing so, we can find out to which element one's ears belong. This in turn may enable one to find out more about one's relation to private and professional happiness as well as more about one's character.

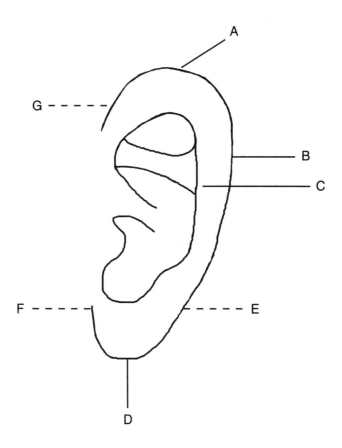

FIGURE 23. The Most Important Points of the Ears

- *B* and *C* point forward, *D* (the earlobe) is tiny, almost not touchable, and the distance between *B* and *G* is significantly longer than between *E* and *F*. The ear is a little bit crooked; its element is wood.

  People with such ears have to work hard throughout their lives. Their social contacts are limited, but there is always enough money for the essentials. They are not especially well suited for family life.

- *A* is pointed and reaches past the end of the eyebrow, *B* and *C* are slanted, and the ear is large, thick, and solid. Its element is fire.

  People with such ears also have to work hard and have a varied life. Even those who attain fame and success will remain alone. The personality is unusual, vain, and not very social.

- *A* is round, *B* and *C* are clearly separated, and *D* is long, soft, and thick. Such ears belong to the element earth; they are large and strong.

  People with such ears can become wealthy, are successful by their own power, and can enrich the family estate (if there is one).

- The line from *B* to *G* is shorter than the line from *E* to *F*. *D* is very long, firm, and soft. *B* and *C* are clearly separated from one another. This ear belongs to the element metal.

  People with such ears have the chance to become rich and famous. These people are very smart; they love the fine arts and have good taste. They are very strong and always keep their composure, but they can be very tender.

- The entire ear is thick, large, soft, and round. *D* lies at the beginning of the neck. The element of this ear is water.

  People of this type are successful without too much effort. They have unusual talents, comprehend things quickly, are decisive, do not take anything too seriously, and are very flexible.

Figure 24. Kwan Shin, Listening to the Internal Voice.

菩
提
葉

FIGURE 25. Pu Ti Jie, Leaves on the Tree of Hope

Wrinkles: "The Erosion of Life"

In ancient China as well as today, elderly people are treated with the highest respect and held in the highest regard—very different from in the West, which has fallen victim to the cult of youth. Old age is always the high point of life, which is why old people should not be pushed into nursing homes but should, as is (still) done in Asia, serve as examples for the entire family. All wise men are depicted as old, for which there is a reason, as is the fact that they always have to exhibit wrinkles. That is why Body Feng Shui teaching says that an old face without wrinkles has bad Feng Shui. Each wrinkle has a special significance, which will now be explained.

Generally speaking the wrinkles around the mouth and chin are easier to spot on men than women. Men that are past thirty but do not yet exhibit those wrinkles that pass downward from the sides of the nose to the corners of the mouth should not be celebrating this fact, since Body Feng Shui teaching states that such men will not reach old age. Normally, these lines should be wide open and clearly marked and go past the corners of the mouth; these types of wrinkles are indicative of a long and healthy life.

生命之紋

FIGURE 26. Shen Ming Tscho Wen, The Erosion of Life

The following drawings depict the five basic types.

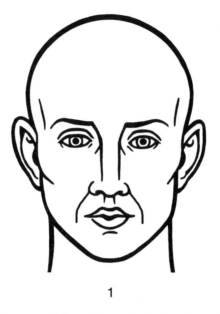

1

1. The wrinkles extend broadly and clearly from the sides of the nose past the corners of the mouth. A sign for happiness and a long life.

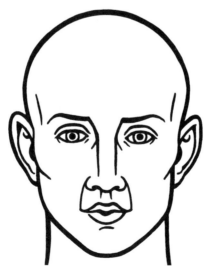

2

2. The wrinkles extend broadly from the sides of the nose exactly
   down to the corners of the mouth. Those with such wrinkles can
   be successful, but may have difficulties in old age.

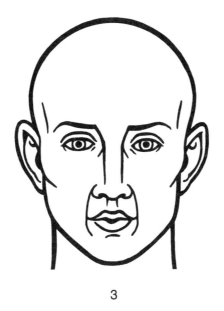

3

3. The wrinkles extend broadly and clearly from the sides of the
   nose exactly down to the corners of the mouth, and from there
   on in a half-moon shape toward the chin. Such wrinkles indicate
   wealth or a long life, but only rarely both together.

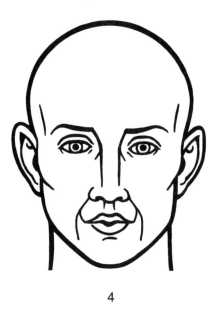

4

4. The wrinkles extend from the sides of the nose to the lips and form a ring; they also come from the sides of the nose down to the chin. Wrinkles of this type indicate that the person will have to deal with social and financial problems.

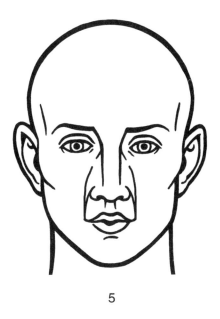

5

5. The wrinkles extend from the sides of the nose to the lips and form a ring; at the same time, two wrinkles extend from the corners of the mouth past the sides of the nose. These types of wrinkles are usually found only among drug addicts or very sick people.

Aside from the cheek and chin wrinkles, great significance is also assigned to the lines on the forehead.

Generally speaking there is nothing bad about lines in the forehead that appear after the age of thirty and run horizontally, as long as they do not cross. However, if they do cross it is a sign for a life full of worries and problems. But if the lines run vertically, the Chinese believe this to mean that the bearer is full of fears. These might be personal or professional.

The following explains the most common vertical shapes of forehead wrinkles.

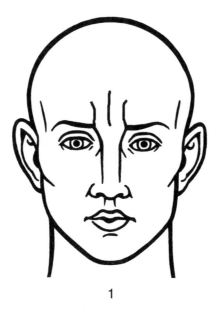

1

1. Two wrinkles extend upward from the eyebrows, with another vertical wrinkle between them. This indicates a large worry that will be present throughout all of life. But if other parts of the face are favorable according to Body Feng Shui teaching, the negative effect of these wrinkles is canceled out.

2. A single wrinkle extends upward right between the eyes. If the wrinkle is not very deep, then it is not a sign of any large damage occurring. But if it is a deep wrinkle, then it means that the life of this person will not be very long; however, if other parts of the face are positive according to Body Feng Shui, they will cancel out the effects of this line.

3. One wrinkle is vertical, and the other resembles a slightly turned L (this might be two lines). Those with such wrinkles will neither be successful nor happy.

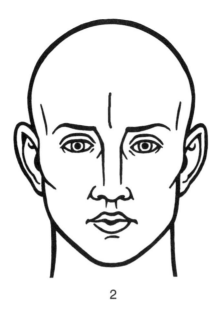

2

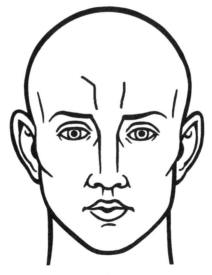

3

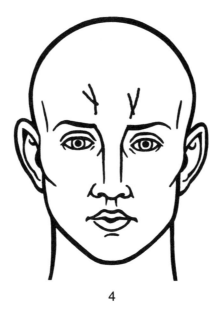

4

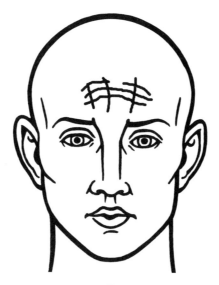

5

4. Double crossed lines on the forehead are an indication of the possibility of an abandoning of family traditions.

5. The grill shape. Those with such wrinkles cannot expect much good in life.

As alluded to in the descriptions of shapes 1 and 2, in Body Feng Shui one always needs to look at the whole picture. This means that everything negative can be balanced out. On the other hand, it also means that positive things can be disturbed.

The Hair: "Clouds in the River of Eternity"

In the Western world men and women often worry a lot about their hairstyles. Of course we admit that a certain hairstyle can significantly influence the personal and professional life of a person, but in the ancient Body Feng Shui teaching it is not hairstyles that are discussed, but the hair itself.

Everybody knows that a hairstyle has to fit with the shape of the face, physique, job, character, and (also somehow) the partner. This is completely right and very important, but more important are the quality of the hair, the quantity of the hair, the color of the hair, the shine of the hair, the direction of growth of the hair, and the overall appearance of body hair in general.

Generally speaking, it can be said that hair should be neither too thin nor too thick, neither too hard nor too soft. Too much is as bad as too little. The direction(s) of hair growth should be clearly recognizable; a mixture, a disorder, indicates unfavorable aspects. The natural color of the hair should be strong; the same goes for its shine. For women it is good if their hair is somewhat finer and softer than the hair of men.

Attention should be paid to the following:

- A very thin person with very thick hair will have a very varied sexual life (even if this is not wanted).

- Someone with thick and rough hair, but who fits the other Body Feng Shui criteria positively, will be successful, in spite or because

FIGURE 27. Tschon, Staying Away from False Things

of the fact that he will have to fight for it. If the other Body Feng Shui criteria (mainly those regarding the face) are not positive, these people will have to work very hard to reach even a minimal level of success. But if this rough and thick hair has a very beautiful color and a nice shine, then success might come more quickly and easily.

- An obese person with thin hair will not have a lot of courage to fight for success; however, this does not mean that she will not be successful.

- The quality of the hair stands in relation to the quality of the skin. The finer the hair, the softer the skin. The rougher the skin, the rougher the hair. Of course, the first case in Body Feng Shui is a positive aspect. The second case is less positive, but does not necessarily have to have a negative influence on life.

- For hairstyles, Body Feng Shui teaching says that the forehead should always be free of hair, because it is considered a symbol for the sunshine of the soul. The cheeks should also not be covered by hair since they are considered the "gates to the soul" and these—same as with a house—should not be permanently shut.

- Women with short hair are—according to the modern Body Feng Shui teaching—open-hearted and independent.

- Women with very short hair often grow up without too much love from their parents, which is why, later in life, they crave attention and love.

- Women with short hair and a perm are often insecure and usually act conservatively in matters of love and life.

FIGURE 28. Scho, To Search for Truth

- Women with shoulder-length hair that is curled inward at the ends care mainly about their looks and often neglect everything else. They appear elegant, but are hard to get along with.

- Women whose long hair is made wavy by using curlers are romantic and desire a comfortable and perfect life, but are not serious. They get what they want, mostly with very little effort.

- Women with very long, wavy hair love a luxurious life and are willing to forfeit deeper studies. They are more interested in details than in the big picture.

- Women with very long, straight hair that is not tied back are tender, goodwilled, and intelligent. They are attracted to love and beauty.

- Women with long hair tied into a braid are considered self-confident, willing to help, smart, and neat. They are open to spiritual matters but not inclined toward social life.

- Women with long hair that is worn pinned up have very good taste. They are elegant, but also arrogant at times.

- Women with gel in their hair are somewhat untidy. They seem friendly, but it is not easy to make friends with them. They are usually more successful in their jobs than in their private lives.

- A hairstyle that covers the forehead can mean that the person is suffering from something that she does not want to reveal. The character of such women is beautiful and tender, even if they often do not look it.

- Hairstyles that cover the cheeks can mean that the person is either very courageous or full of self-doubt. These women give the impression of accomplishing extraordinary things, which is true, but at the same time a deep-rooted fear is constantly present. They often have problems with every type of partnership.

FIGURE 29. Shan, To Follow Nature

- Hairstyles that are combed from the middle indicate that the person is honest, courageous, and realistic.

- Hairstyles that are combed to the side reveal a romantic tendency.

- Women who wear their hair only combed back do not always show their true feelings. Nonetheless, they still have a noble character and a lot of understanding for children.

- Western women who prefer African hairstyles are constantly looking for new things and love to make their own decisions. They easily master difficult situations.

When one speaks of hair, one should not forget that a beard consists of hair, too, and thus also receives attention in Body Feng Shui, especially because it is closely linked with the sex hormone testosterone, which enhances beard growth among men.

The male beard grows especially in three spots: on the chin, between the nose and lips, and on the cheeks. It is good when the regions a full beard covers are still clearly recognizable. But if everything grows wildly, the hair will surround the mouth like a circle. Body Feng Shui regards the mouth as the entrance for luck, and understandably this entrance should not be blocked. The quality of the facial hair should be the same as that of the head hair, and the same goes for quantity. Too little beard means that the person is not able to be independently successful, even though he has enough talent. Too much beard indicates that the person is very active in love matters. He also has a lot of courage but is not very careful. Thin beard hair shows that the owner is tender, but full of doubt. Such people can be successful in their youth, but their strength does not suffice to keep up the success; they need the help of others for this. People with thick facial hair are often impatient, and their lives are constantly going up and down.

FIGURE 30. Yun Bin, Clouds in the River of Eternity

When talking about hair, one of course cannot ignore the hair that one does not see at first glance—body and pubic hair, the latter of which is of greater importance with women than it is with men.

For both types of hair, the same criteria apply as for the head hair. For pubic hair in particular, the following also applies: it can provide information about health; it tells of one's relation to love; it indicates intelligence; and it can illuminate a personality.

The following drawings indicate the six basic shapes.

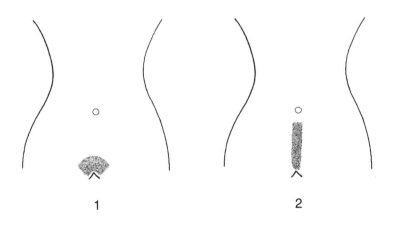

1. This shape is the best. The entire circulatory system works very well; the person is in excellent health. The bearer is tender and understanding, has a good personality and a high IQ, and can be a great mother.

2. This shape is less favorable. Women with this type of hair are often shy and insecure; they have less of a sex drive and are more vulnerable to illnesses. Although they are eager to learn, they are not of very high intelligence.

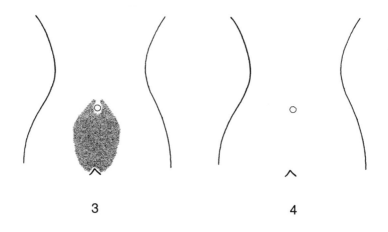

3   4

3. This shape is also less favorable. Women of this type are often impulsive, restless, impatient, and hungry for love. They have their own set of morals, and usually a rather adventurous job.

4. This shape is very rare and is called the "white tiger" in China. Women who never develop any hair are not very successful, have little chance in a relationship, are often ill, and lack courage.

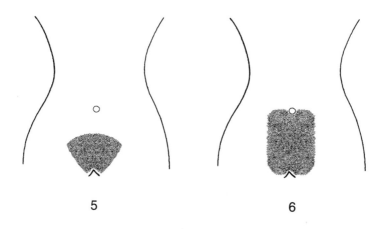

5   6

5. This shape is neither very positive nor negative; in other words, it is a neutral shape. Women with this type of pubic hair have a temper and are dominating. They want to completely control their

partner and children. Yet at the same time they are very responsible, reliable, and careful. This type of woman is usually in good health.

6. This shape is less positive. This type of woman is usually overeager, loves constant change, and rarely cares about others. Even if they are not very intelligent, they have a lot of courage. They are generous in financial affairs.

The Hands: "The Way to the Heart"

Whenever there is talk of hands and their special significance, we tend to look at the lines in our palms and their interpretations. But these interpretations are—at least partly—unreliable, especially because these lines keep changing throughout life, even though the changes are small. Therefore, the shape of the hands, fingers, and fingernails is more important than the lines of our palms. Maybe a compromise can be found using a comparison: The hand itself is the territory, the lines of the palm are the house; both belong together. In ancient Body Feng Shui, however, the territory is regarded as being more important, which is why we learn nothing about the house. Maybe this is because one can study the shape of someone's hand at all times and without problems, while this is not possible with the palm.

Generally speaking, the shape of hands too can be accorded to the five elements (wood, fire, earth, metal, water), but in addition there is a sixth shape, a combination of the five elements. This shape will be discussed later.

A good hand should be firm and strong, the skin should be slightly shiny, and the fingers should be of the same quality and consistency, with the thumb being stronger than the rest so that the hand is in harmony. According to this harmony, it is advantageous if a long hand also exhibits long fingers and nails and a short one has shorter fingers and nails. If the hand looks too bony, soft, loose, wrinkled, fat, or disproportional, then its Body Feng Shui too is unfavorable and sooner or later there will be problems.

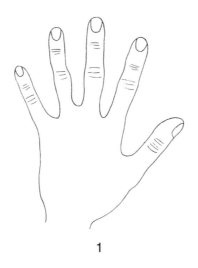

1

The following diagrams show the five basic hand shapes.

1. This shape appears especially among people who work predominantly with their heads. The inside appears flat, and the region between the wrist and the fingers is mostly longer than the fingers themselves. The flesh in this region is neither too firm nor too soft, but strong. Fingers and nails are long and look elegant. The skin at the joints of the fingers is slightly wrinkled, the tips of the fingers are neither round nor pointed, and the thumb is very strong and cannot be bent backward.

   People with this type of hand are usually intellectually talented. Whatever happens, their mind will be able to analyze the situation. They are very patient and able to deal with setbacks. They have a lot of endurance, and while they do not ignore money, they are not cheap either. Such people usually have an idealistic personality. They have a great liking for art and great taste, even though they at times appear to be too much in love with details. In the five-element teaching the element wood belongs to this hand.

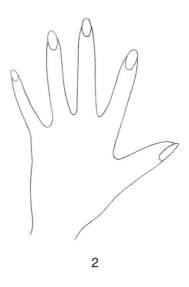

2

2. This strangely shaped hand appears among people who are very romantic or idealistic. This hand is very long and extremely beautiful and fine. It may be the most beautiful of all shapes. The palms are not too fleshy, but are also not bony. The tips are pointed and the skin on the joints exhibits very few wrinkles. This hand is elegant, noble, and aesthetic, but its owners, unfortunately, are usually just the opposite. Whatever happens, positive or negative, these people quickly lose their calm, but also regain it quickly. They have excellent taste, but their thoughts race along like wild horses. That is why their ideas rarely turn into deeds. Such people tend to be very dependent on others and often have to trust and work with others. Whenever they can summon the energy to do something, it is not planned ahead of time, but simply begun; that is why success is rare for them. In the five-element teaching the element fire belongs to this hand.

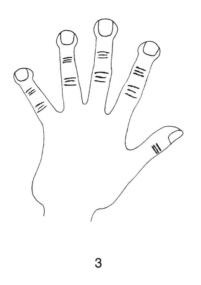

3

3. This shape, called "pioneer hand," is oval, and the flesh is especially firm and strong; it is a hardworking hand. The outer line is not clearly defined, but exhibits occasional curves. The wrist is very small, which makes the hand seem larger. The fingers seem long and broad and the tips are flat and geckolike; they remind one of small suction cups.

   People with these hands are very enduring; they react quickly, are full of physical strength, and are rarely tired. They are considered to be good at manual tasks and have the courage to admit to what they do. They are trustworthy, openhearted, and friendly. They do not care about appearances and neither are they vain nor do they like to show off. Their talents and their strength often tempt them to break with tradition. They like to speak their mind and usually believe that they are the only ones who are right, which is why they are quickly enraged, and it is hard to change their mind. Such people like to be independent, and if they are lucky they can make it far. In the five-element teaching the element earth belongs to this hand.

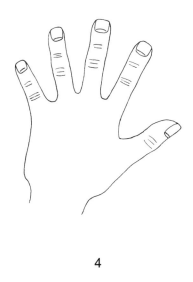

4

4. This hand is also called "the square." It is a hand that works hard and is very realistic. The insides are very firm, but the flesh is tender. The nails are rather short, as are the fingers. The tips and nails are square. The thumb is very pronounced.

People with this type of hand are very realistic and accurately observe daily events and world news. They avoid spending money on anything "inessential," which is why they do not have any hobbies. They are very smart and patient. In regard to their family they watch money closely (in the good sense) and do not require any unnecessary luxury. They blindly obey orders without questioning them. They are very straightforward. In the five-element teaching the element metal belongs to this hand.

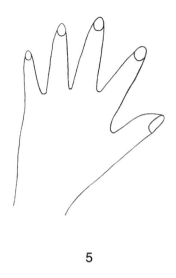

5

5. This hand is round, very fleshy, and very soft. Wrinkles on the joints are hard to make out. The fingers resemble inverted ice-cream cones. Nails as well as fingertips are round, but have a small tip.

   People with this type of hand are talented in arts and crafts. They have a good heart and are very sentimental. They often change their point of view and do not have great staying power, which is why they often give up halfway. When men have such hands, they are a sign of eloquence, sensitivity, and understanding. Women with this type of hand are vain, have little staying power, and are not very strong. They have no problems, however, in matters of love. They can be very tricky in order to attain their goals. In the five-element teaching the element water belongs to this hand.

6. This is the shape that cannot be pictured, because as a mixture, it has infinite possibilities. To determine the character of this hand it is necessary to find out which element of the five-element teaching is most prevalent. After that one can take the appropriate description from shapes 1 through 5.

What has been said so far is always helpful when one wants to judge the character and personality of a person, which is the purpose of the Body Feng Shui teaching. It is especially necessary when one meets a person whose face exhibits no deviation from the norm.

One should never forget, however, that everything about a person plays a role, and it would be a mistake to draw conclusions from details. It is necessary to keep in mind the big picture, which is why Body Feng Shui is so complex. With Feng Shui, which deals with living, it is also important to regard the whole in order then to assign equal significance to details. People who are able to accomplish this have mastered the secret of harmony. With Feng Shui there are numerous aids to deter bad things or to fix them, and the same exists with Body Feng Shui; but here it is not visible, because it is one's own soul, one's one heart, and one's inner self.

Although the hand as a whole plays a pivotal role in Body Feng Shui, the significance of the individual fingers should not be ignored.

FIGURE 31. Shin, The Inner Self

Considered the most important digit, the thumb should have

- the right position, meaning that the tip of the thumb should extend to the level indicated in figure 32;
- a straight build;
- and it should not be possible to bend back the entire thumb.

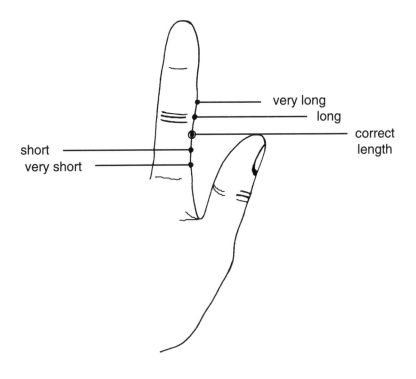

FIGURE 32. The Proper Thumb

People with strong thumbs of the right length and of a beautiful build rarely change their opinions and do not give up easily. They have kind hearts and are friendly, smart, and astute in business matters.

People with thumbs that are too long are often predisposed toward manual tasks, have very high self-esteem, and are extremely stubborn. But if the rest of the hand has good Body Feng Shui, this person is capable of extraordinary things.

People with short thumbs are easily influenced, are rarely eager or able to learn new things, and always recognize when they have an advantage. But if the rest of the hand has good Body Feng Shui, such a person can react well and positively to all changes in life.

Generally speaking, the thumb is divided into three parts: from the tip to the first joint, from the first joint to the second, and from the second joint to the mount of Venus. The first part represents wishes, hopes, and desires; the second part the ability for logical and rational thought. These two parts thus have to do with the mind. The third part, in contrast, has to do with the body, as the mount of Venus gives information about the libido of the person.

All three parts should be in harmony with one another with regard to their position, firmness, and stability. For a better understanding, here is a guide to nine thumb types.

1. If the extended thumb forms a perfectly straight line, this means that the person has a very steady character, thinks ahead, and is not easily deterred. On the other hand, the person can be stubborn and egotistical.

2. If the extended thumb forms a perfectly straight line in which the first part is bent slightly outward, this means that the person has very good judgment. Such a person never suffers from doubts before making a decision, but is always willing to listen to tips and advice from others. This person is generous but does not waste money.

3. If the extended thumb has a perfect outward bend, it means that the person is very sensitive. She gets along with everybody and is smart, understanding, and forgiving. Her emotions are always written on her face. Such people tend to waste money.

4. If the extended thumb bends inward, one can assume that the bearer is not going to change his opinions. Such a person will insist on his point of view and not give others credit. He is very egotistical, even in regard to his family. He sticks to the law and is very controlled.

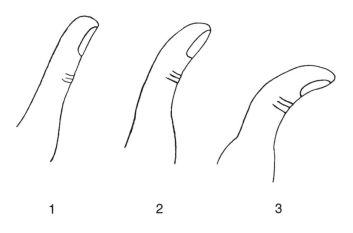

1   2   3

5. If the thumb in its extended state has a very close connection to the index finger this means that the person rarely develops her own ideas. She is dependent on the creativity of others and is conservative and miserly.

6. A long distance between the extended thumb and the index finger means that the person has a character of extremes. He likes to appear relaxed, but is only pretending. A person of this type is not able to judge the consequences of his actions. He is, however, always willing to help and very giving.

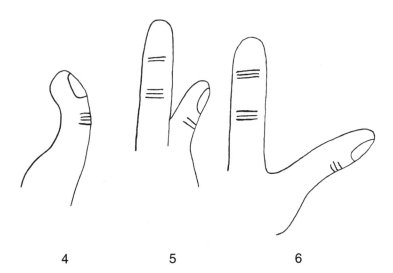

4   5   6

7. If the first part of the thumb is especially thin, this indicates mood swings and indecisiveness as well as a desire to control from above.

8. If the tip of the thumb is very round, this indicates a person who prefers being physical and athletic to pursuing intellectual occupations. She can be easily enraged, which can lead to big problems.

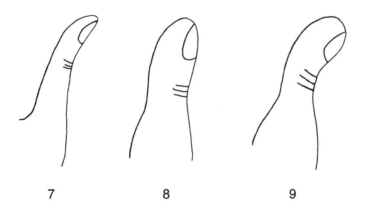

7   8   9

9. If the middle of the thumb is thinner than the two other parts, this indicates a very high level of physical and mental activity. The sense of justice is limited among these people, however.

Considering that we have ten fingers, it is surprising that the thumb has six-tenths of the strength of all the fingers. The remaining four-tenths remain for the other fingers. For favorable Body Feng Shui these other fingers also have to be in harmony. Thus the following apply:

- the index finger should reach the midpoint of the first part of the middle finger;

- the middle finger does not have to adhere to any size norm and stands by itself;

- the tip of the ring finger should slightly pass the midpoint of the first part of the middle finger;

- the tip of the pinkie should coincide with the first line (from the top) of the ring finger.

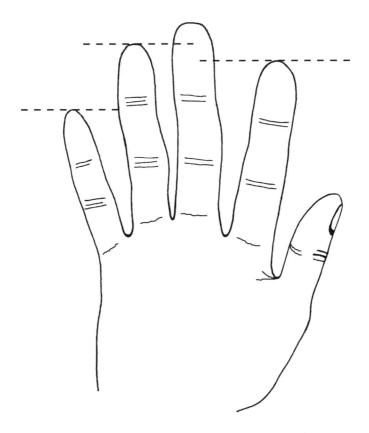

FIGURE 33. Finger Proportions

About the significance of the individual fingers, the following can be said:

- The index finger gives information on the self-esteem of a person. If the finger is straight and strong and of the right length, then the person is intelligent and brave. If the finger is longer than normal, the person likes to dominate—the longer the finger, the more hungry for power the person will be. If the index finger is too short, the person may be without courage and shy away from responsibility. If the fingertip appears to be square, this bespeaks a realistic person. If it is pointed, the person is religious. If the tip is oval, the person is curious. If the index finger stands far apart from the middle finger, this indicates an open mind.

- The middle finger indicates how a person thinks about life itself. If this finger is of the right length and is straight and strong, the person is considerate, understanding, and forward-looking. Such a person is always friendly and considerate. If this finger is long and wide and thus looks oversized, this speaks of attentiveness, melancholy, and a very sentimental nature. If the finger is too short, this person has no opinion of his own, has mood swings, and is easily influenced. If the fingertip appears pointed, it is a sign of a disorderly nature and one lacking a sense of responsibility. If the tip is square, this indicates a serious personality. An oval shape indicates a soft heart. If the middle finger is very close to the index finger, this indicates blind faith and obedience. If it is too close to the ring finger, this person is generous.

- According to Body Feng Shui, artistic talent is found in the ring finger. If the ring finger is of the right length and strong, this means that the person has good taste, a positive character, and much talent for arts and crafts. If the finger is too long, this person has an outstanding talent for an art; however, such people are also always looking for an advantage and do not accept being second to anybody. If the ring finger is too short, the person has a unique taste. A pointed fingertip indicates mild hysteria, a square one a stable character. If the tip is oval, it speaks of endurance and a brilliant artistic career. If the ring finger is very far from the middle finger, it means that the person is not able to judge the consequences of her actions. If the finger is very close to the middle finger, it means that the person is very old-fashioned.

- The pinkie shows someone's talent for scientific work as well as talent in business matters and the ability for public speaking. If the finger is of the right length and strong, this indicates intelligence and good business manners. If the finger is a little long, this indicates an interest in thinking. Such people are often very successful. If the finger is a little shorter, this indicates a serious character, which will also lead to success. But if the finger is short and weak, this indicates self-esteem problems, an inability to deal with money, and little intelligence. But if such a finger is found on an otherwise perfect hand, it is possible that these negative characteristics do not show. A person with a pointed tip is very interested in science. An oval shape indicates a talent for business, and a square shape a healthy sense of reality. If the pinkie is very close to the ring finger, this indicates a preference for some type of art; if it is far from the ring finger, this suggests a very careful person who is prepared for all possibilities.

The following descriptions apply to the shape of the hand, especially of the fingers together.

- People with long fingers care more about spiritual matters than material things. They take into account details, are very neat, and are very interested in everything that is happening.

- People with short fingers are very materialistic and do not like to deal with spiritual matters. They are full of courage, only rarely regret an action, and are very decisive; they are often impatient.

- People with fingers that are bent slightly inward (regardless of whether the fingers are long or short) think clearly and carefully, and look ahead.

- People with fingers that are bent slightly outward have a friendly and warm personality and are very curious, but also diplomatic.

With regard to the joints:

- If the skin covering the joints is very wrinkled, this indicates a smart, logical person who is very organized. This person looks ahead and does not do anything before having ascertained that the result will be positive.

- If no wrinkles are showing, this indicates people who do not make decisions with their minds, but rather with their hearts. They are very flexible, good-natured, and friendly, but they give up easily.

Now let us discuss the insides of the hands. In Body Feng Shui the "mounts" (sometimes called "hills") that can be found there are of greater significance than the lines on our palms (see figure 34). There are ten of these "mounts," and each has a special significance that we shall now explain.

Mount A: This mount should be firm and not too high. This indicates politeness, tenderness, generosity, and fairness. People with such a (Venus) mount are very sensitive. If the mount is too high, the owners have troubles taming their sexual appetites. If it is too flat, the sexual appetite is very reduced.

Mount B: This mount too should be fleshy and not too high. People with such mounts are very well coordinated and creative; they are well suited for artistic jobs. If the mount is too high, this could indicate a loss of reality. If it is too flat, this indicates a lack of creativity and an egotistical personality.

Mount C: If this mount is positive (as described for mounts *A* and *B*), it indicates honesty, trust, and positive thinking. People with this constellation like fame, but do not desire it. If the mount is

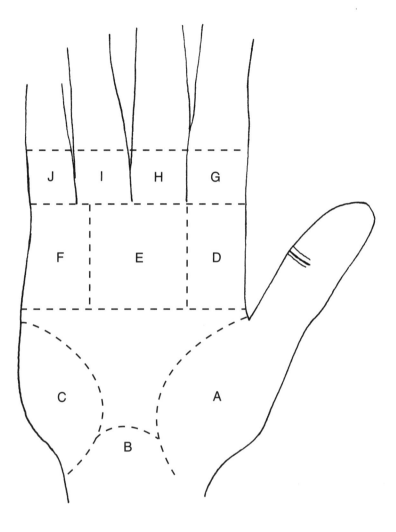

FIGURE 34. The Ten Mounts of the Palm

too high, this reveals ambition and arrogance. If it is too flat, there is a lack of courage and talent.

Mount D: Should be fleshy and not too high. People of this type are very stable and eager to learn. They get along with everybody.

If the mount is too high, they are lonely and nervous; if the mount is too flat, they are boring and lack taste.

Mount E: Should also be fleshy and not too high. This indicates a tender personality and absolute honesty. Such a person is full of energy and is artistically talented. A mount that is too high indicates a character who likes an adventurous but luxurious life. If the mount is too flat, the owner is only concerned with the material aspects of life.

Mount F: If this mount is perfect its owner has great talent for scientific work and for business of every kind. He is willing to engage in dialogue and should not suffer from any financial worries. If the mount is too high, this indicates a low willingness to learn. If the mount is too flat, there might be financial difficulties.

Mount G: In the best case scenario, this mount should not be high, but rather flat. This indicates self-control, courage, an adventurous nature, and the ability to adapt to changing circumstances. However, if the mount is very high, this person is rather uncontrolled, is always looking out for her own interests, and is ready to take advantage of others. If the mount is too flat, this indicates an inability to make the best of a situation and a lack of courage.

Mount H: Should be like mount G. Indicates clear thinking, a lot of courage, and a person who can deal with any situation. A mount that is too high indicates an increase of these characteristics; a mount that is too flat indicates a lack of courage, indecisiveness, and an inability to see things through.

Mount I: This mount should be slightly curved, for then it indicates great talent in business or politics. People of this type are physically and mentally very active and have a temper. If the mount is too high, it indicates business manners that are not always correct. If the mount is too low, these people have troubles finding the meaning of life.

Mount J: Should be fleshy, neither too high nor too flat. People with such a mount are very mild and careful; they do not show

FIGURE 35. Shan Gan, Sensuousness

off and will not give up. If the mount is too high, the person is only out for his or her own good and is also impatient. If the mount is too flat, it indicates nervousness, unfounded fears, and a lack of energy.

Unfortunately, people cannot influence their mounts, in contrast to their nails. All women who care about their appearance take special care of their nails, something that men have increasingly started doing as well. Even in ancient China there was a beauty treatment for nails: a dye was extracted from flower petals and applied to the nails—the predecessor of the modern nail polish, which has been enhanced today by nail accessories as well as manicures, which often remove the small white skin that connects the nail with the finger to make the nail appear even larger and more perfect in shape. This procedure carries risks, because it opens up possibilities for bacteria to enter the body and cause infections. Nail polish, furthermore, has as a drawback the fact that the nail is unable to breathe. In addition, it should be noted that nails become darker as one goes down the evolutionary ladder. The higher-ranking the species, the lighter are the nails; thus one has to ask oneself why women are consciously trying to place themselves on a lower level.

In Body Feng Shui, fingernails provide information about health, character, and personality of a person. Generally speaking, the nails should be in harmony with the finger and the hand in general. The color should be light rose, and the surface should be smooth. If this is the case, the owner is generally in good health. The following drawings and explanations provide other details.

1. The nail is narrow and long. This means that the body by nature is weak and sickly. Furthermore, people with these types of nails are very jealous.

2. The nail is short and rectangular. Its owner is strong and full of energy. People with these types of nails are friendly.

3. The nail is round. Such people have a large reservoir of the element fire. They are quickly enraged but easily appeased.

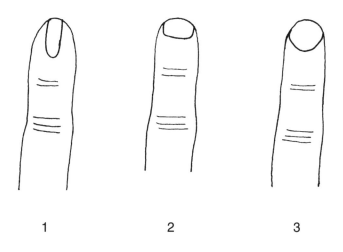

4. Oval shape. People with such nails have good taste and always look for the nicer things in life.

5. The nail is wider at the top than at the bottom. This indicates good taste and quick understanding, but it also bespeaks a lack of courage.

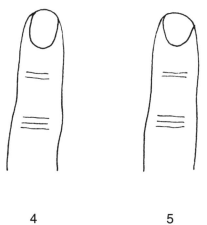

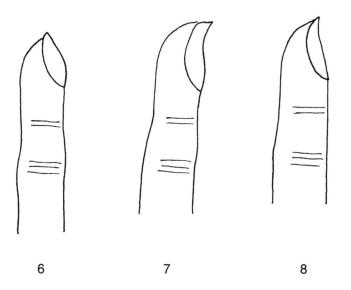

6   7   8

6. The nail is curved downward too much. People with such nails tend to have breathing problems.

7. The nail is bent upward too much; liver or lung problems are probable.

8. The outer tip is bent upward: there may be problems with the liver, kidneys, or genitals.

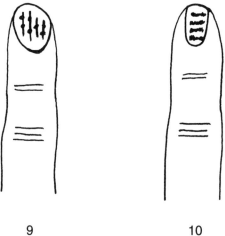

9   10

9. There are spotted vertical lines on the nail. This indicates stomach and nerve problems.

10. There are horizontal lines on the nail, a sign of possible intestinal problems.

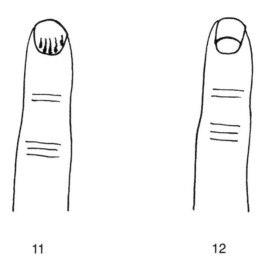

11   12

11. Lines in the lower part of the nail are a further indication of a disturbance in the general nervous system.

12. The "moon" should be neither too big nor too small; too big indicates a risk of high blood pressure, too small indicates low blood pressure.

After these various examinations of the hand, a short demystification of the three most important palm lines is necessary—without succumbing to fortune-telling at this point. In general, the following considerations apply: If the lines are in harmony with one another, the hand itself will also be well shaped. The opposite is not always the case. The lines themselves, however, are not always set; they change according to the period and circumstances in life, and the lines of the left hand are different from the lines of the right hand. For this reason alone, it is very doubtful that three lines could tell the entire life of a person.

We generally differentiate between three main lines (see figure 36):

A, which encircles the mount of Venus, is the health and life line;

B, which runs across the palm, is the line of intelligence, and is also called the career line;

C, which is closest to the fingers, is responsible for love.

For the A line the following apply: If it runs in an oval curve toward the wrist and is deep and clearly recognizable, this indicates health, positive thinking, creativity, and empathy. Yet if it runs straight

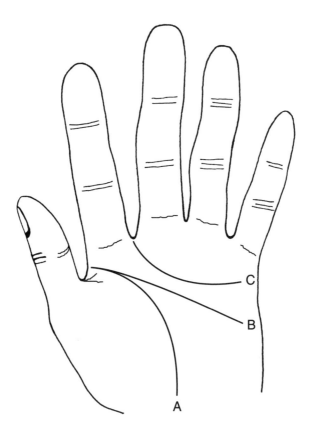

FIGURE 36. The Three Lines of Fate

toward the wrist, it reveals a lack of self-control. If it is a double line, it indicates great physical energy, honesty, and an uncontrolled temper.

For the *B* line the following apply: If it starts at the origin of the *A* line and clearly crosses the palm, then the person is very intelligent, decisive, and very well suited to deal with finances. If this line starts at a different point, the person is very clever, tough, and quickly enraged. If the line runs straight toward the wrist, then it indicates artistic talent as well as the realistic assessment of situations. If the line is curved upward, it is a good sign for any type of enterprise or job.

And for the *C* line, the following apply: If it is more clearly defined than the *B* line, it indicates that feelings are stronger than reason, and melancholy might be a problem. If the line runs very close to the fingers, it indicates an uncontrolled temper. If it is lower, the person is miserly. If it appears long, the owner is often blind in matters of love, which is why he is exposed to much suffering. If it is very short, it indicates egotism. If the *C* line is broken, this is never a condition from birth (as with the two other lines), but is always because of a former, and large, problem in love.

To close this discussion, I would like to add some other basic considerations about the language of hands. These are often expressed in the following habits:

- *Hands in the pockets:* People who do this permanently want to be considered unapproachable, consider themselves to be something special, and want to hide weaknesses.

- *Hands crossed in front of the chest:* This means that the person does not want to have anything to do with the other and is not open to foreign influences.

- *Hands pressed together while speaking:* A sign of great stress and nervousness.

- *Hands dangling at the sides:* A clear sign of calm, laziness, or untidiness.

- *Hands constantly reaching for something:* A person with this habit is very stressed and impatient.

FIGURE 37. Wuo Shao, To Extend One's Hand to Someone

- *Hands rubbing against one another:* Anticipation of coming positive events.

- *Fingers are bent forward one after another, until they make a sound:* These people are full of worries and unrest.

- *Hands on hips:* Indicates an overestimation of oneself.

- *Hiding fingers in the mouth:* Indicates dishonesty or faked interest.

There are also physically based characteristics with hands that have a special meaning. Among these are:

- *Sweat:* People with sweaty hands are very nervous and in bad health.

- *The palms are rose or yellow and shiny:* This indicates good health, a happy character, and excellent brain activity.

- *The palms are dark red:* People with these palms have an extreme character and lack all self-control.

- *The palms are brown:* The person has worries in her life.

- *The palms look white (not because of an illness):* A sign of egotism, a loveless character, and incomprehension.

The Voice: "The Song of the Nightingale"

The quality of a person can be heard in the quality of his or her voice, even though, of course, there are differences between male and female voices. The male voice should be strong, the female voice soft. But if the male voice is strong, but also rough, dry, and cracking, then this person will obviously have less success in relationships and business than someone whose voice is deep but smooth. The same applies to the female voice: If it is soft, but without shine, clarity, or inner strength, its owner will have more problems in life than a person who has a clear, soft, tender, but strong voice.

The strength of a voice does not come from the lips or the throat, but from the diaphragm, as every opera singer knows, which is why they practice diaphragmatic breathing. This type of breathing was known to the Taoist sages, who used this type of breathing to meditate and to revitalize themselves and believed that it helped in prolonging life. But not even this is enough for a perfect voice. Body Feng Shui teaching says that the voice should also correspond with one's element (see the first chapter to find your element):

Wood: The voice should be high-pitched, clear, and shiny.
Fire: A strong and slightly dry voice would be appropriate.
Earth: A deep and voluminous voice is very favorable.
Metal: This voice should be mild and smooth.
Water: For good Body Feng Shui the voice should be clear and rhythmical.

If the voice is in harmony with the elements, this will help one to lead a successful life; however, if this is not the case, any weakness can certainly be compensated by other, positive, Body Feng Shui characteristics.

FIGURE 38. Wan Tschoan Huang In, The Song of the Nightingale

The Cheeks: "Pillows of Power"

In ancient China, the same word was used for "cheeks" and "power," which explains why the cheeks are of such importance in Body Feng Shui. What is decisive is not their size, but their fullness and their proportion to the ears and nose. Figure 39 shows a well-proportioned face.

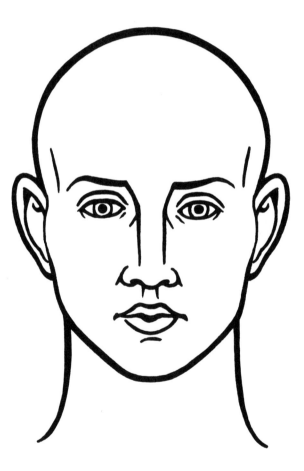

FIGURE 39. Good Cheek Position

This cheek position is advantageous because the cheeks extend from the nose to the sides but do not touch the lower corners of the eye. Furthermore, they are fleshy, the cheekbones are not visible, and they do not go past the ridge of the nose. People with such cheeks will be masters and never servants. Figure 40 depicts a different situation.

This cheek position will be disadvantageous because the cheeks are much too close to the lower corners of the eyes, and because the bones are visible owing to the height of the cheeks. Such cheeks will exercise a bad influence on one's marriage, sex life, and love life.

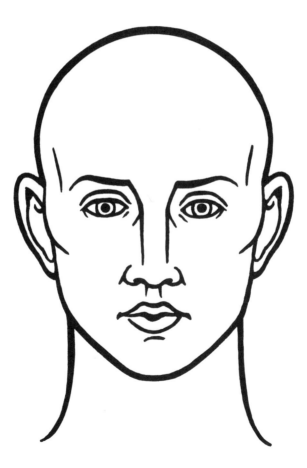

FIGURE 40. Bad Cheek Position 1

Figure 41 shows a position that is equally disadvantageous. This cheek position is disadvantageous because the cheeks extend from the nose to the middle of the ear. Here, neither the cheekbones nor the cheeks themselves are clearly visible. People with such cheeks do not aim for higher things, have no courage, and have no power. In China one would say that "such a person wants to eat, but not grow anything."

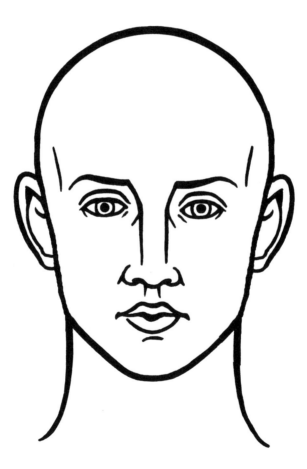

FIGURE 41. Bad Cheek-Position 2

Figure 42. Tschuen Tschon, Pillows of Power

The Forehead: "The Hills of Wisdom"

According to Body Feng Shui the forehead should occupy one-third of the face. It should be slightly curved and not appear too fleshless.

Generally, it can be said that a high forehead indicates intelligence, while a low one indicates strong doubt. A forward-curving forehead tells of courage but a lack of attention; a small, straight forehead indicates a lack of intelligence.

Five parts can be identified on a forehead that provide information about the fate of the owner. These illustrate the influence of one's parents, one's personal development, and one's relations with colleagues, with society, and to material goods. Figure 43 indicates where these five parts are located.

> *The significance of A:* The paternal influence during childhood. If it was positive, this area will not be covered by hair; it will also not be hilly.

> *The significance of B:* The maternal influence during childhood. If positive, this part will not be hilly; it will also not have any marks.

> *The significance of C:* Personal development. If positive, we find neither hills nor tiny valleys, neither spots nor marks.

> *The significance of D:* Relations with other people. If positive, the same applies as for A to C.

> *The significance of E:* The relationship to the material world. If positive, this part should not be covered by the eyebrows. At the same time it is advantageous if the distance between the eyebrows is neither too large nor too small.

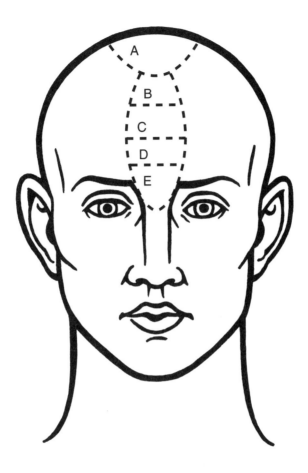

FIGURE 43. The Five Most Important Parts of the Forehead

智慧之頂

FIGURE 44. Tsche Huei Tsche Ding, The Hill of Wisdom

The Chin: "The Source of Eternal Life"

As with the forehead, the chin (together with the part between the nose and lips) should also make up one-third of the face.

The chin is the end of the face; it is the point at which all lines meet. That is why in Body Feng Shui it stands for the knowledge of what will occur in the later years of our lives.

In figure 45, four zones are differentiated on the chin: zone *A* represents the luck that is brought to one by the following generations; zone *B* (the lower lip) gives information about the mature personality of a person; zone *C* concerns financial circumstances; and zone *D* speaks to health and life expectancy.

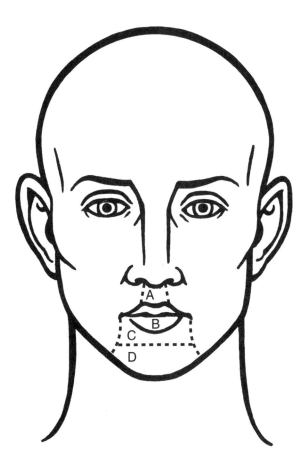

FIGURE 45. The Four Most Important Parts of the Chin

The significance of zone A: The happiness that is brought to one by children and grandchildren. It is advantageous if this region is exactly in the middle between the nose and lips and is in a deep, clear, straight line. The upper part of the "valley" should be a bit narrower than the lower part.

The significance of zone B: The mature character, inner values. It is good if this zone is in harmony with the upper lip and the rest of the face. For men the lower lip should be slightly thinner than the upper lip. For women the opposite applies.

The significance of zone C: Financial circumstances, external values. It is favorable if this part is set back a little, but not too far, as otherwise the positive will turn into its opposite.

The significance of zone D: Health and life expectancy. It is advantageous if this part has a clear shape, which should not be too pointed. There can be some flesh, so that the bone is not too visible. A valley tells of an unsteady life, which can be quite long.

不朽之源

FIGURE 46. Bu Schiu Tsche Yuen, The Source of Eternal Life

Beauty Marks: "Buds of Eternal Spring"

By beauty marks we mean birthmarks, moles, and red dots of *natural* origin. If the marks are visible at first glance, this is negative, unless they are red or black, which is positive. Figure 47 shows preferred spots for beauty marks, which are mostly negative (unless they are red or black).

For an explanation of the various points, the following list is provided.

> *Point 1:* It is difficult to get help from others. Men have problems with their fathers, women with their partners.

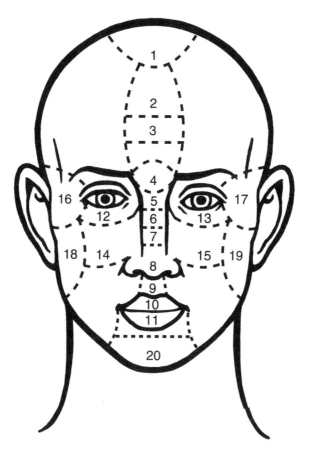

FIGURE 47. Preferred Locations for Beauty Marks

Point 2: Men rarely receive help from their parents, women are dominated by their partners.

Point 3: Same as point 2.

Point 4: There can be problems with the inheritance. There is also too much of a willingness to give in.

Point 5: Marital problems and problems with love in general are possible.

Point 6: Health problems have to be anticipated.

Point 7: Same as point 6.

Point 8: Problems are caused by the partner.

Point 9: Problems with the children and with health.

Point 10: There will never be any intestinal problems.

Point 11: The opposite of point 10 will occur.

Point 12: No connection with children.

Point 13: Same as point 12.

Point 14: There is the possibility of a loss of power.

Point 15: Same as point 14.

Point 16: Love behavior can become very unsteady.

Point 17: Same as point 16.

Point 18: Things that are started are rarely finished.

Point 19: Same as point 18.

Point 20: It is better to be independent than to want to continue family traditions.

To the Western reader this section might seem somewhat incredible or even ridiculous. In Asia, however, it is the norm to consult with a Body Feng Shui expert before removing a beauty mark and to discuss the positive and negative effects of the mark.

萬

春

蓓

蕾

FIGURE 48. Wan Tschuen Pei Lei, Buds of Eternal Spring

FIGURE 49. Chi Fu Shin, The Pleiades of Happiness

The Back of the Head: "The Pleiades of Happiness"

If one wants to describe an unusual or a great personality in China, one says, "The back of their head is full of corners." Apparently, this part of the human body is of special interest, and many Body Feng Shui experts in the past have said that they only need to feel the back of someone's head to determine the fate and personality of a person. The zones of the back of head that they examine for this should be round and easily grasped, since this indicates positive Body Feng Shui.

Figure 50 shows the locations of these zones.

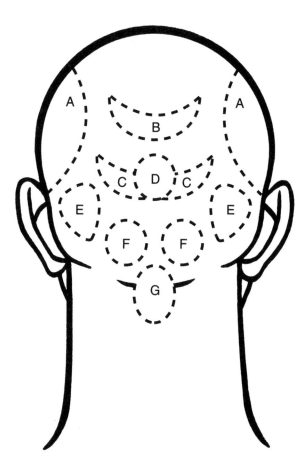

FIGURE 50. Zones of the Back of the Head

If the Body Feng Shui of the back of the head is positive, the following interpretations derive from the various zones:

Zone A: The person is very intelligent and will be successful.

Zone B: This often indicates luck in financial affairs.

Zone C: This person is very intelligent and can become rich and famous.

Zone D: Unusual fame and wealth can be expected.

Zone E: This person will have a long life and survive misfortune without harm.

Zone F: Called the "twin dragon." It guarantees a long life, fame, and wealth.

Zone G: The person will be successful, even if her personality is somewhat odd.

The Breasts: "The Petals of Reincarnation"

Nature has created two genders, but only one of them received the wonderful present of breasts. Breasts feed life, and they feed lust; this already makes them more than unusual. Although almost everybody values large and full breasts, this says nothing about their quality. That is why there is a separate Body Feng Shui section for breasts, which is derived from ancient knowledge. Here the question is not full or big or sexy, but whether the shape is in proportion to other body parts and thereby creates a positive Body Feng Shui.

The following diagrams show the twelve main breast shapes; each of their characteristics is explained to make it clear that no shape is exclusively positive or negative, but rather that it is important to make the right choice when choosing a partner. A partner should always complement a person, and the choice should never be made based on a wrong ideal.

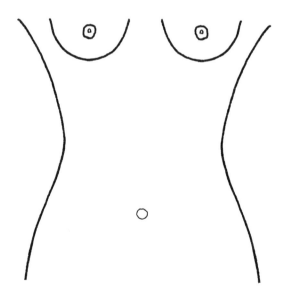

1

Shape 1: "The rice bowls." This shape rises as a hill on the rib cage. It is very full, but not unusually large. In the teachings of Body Feng Shui this shape is regarded as one of the most beautiful. Women with such breasts are very healthy and have an open heart. If their breasts are firm, they are responsible with money and have a love life that is free of problems. If the breasts are soft, money tends to be wasted and sexual interest is rather low, but at the same time this woman will be a loving partner and mother.

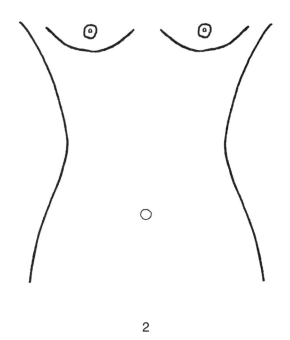

2

Shape 2: "The plates of jade." This shape rises only slightly from the rib cage. These women have a noble, reserved personality. They are often shy and conservative, but full of thoughts. That is also why physical interests rank below spiritual interests for them. Nonetheless they have very erotic tendencies, which of course do not necessarily have to be acted upon.

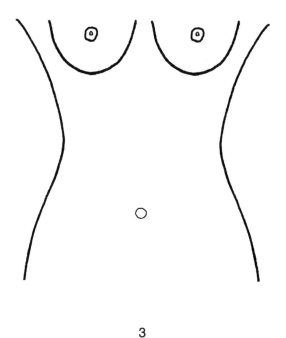

3

Shape 3: "The family rice bowls." Very similar to shape 1, except that here the breasts rise much higher. Women with such breasts have a very healthy love life and can give birth to healthy children, which, however, does not necessarily mean that they will be good mothers. This is because they often place their own interests first. If the nipples are very large, they do not have a lot of self-control.

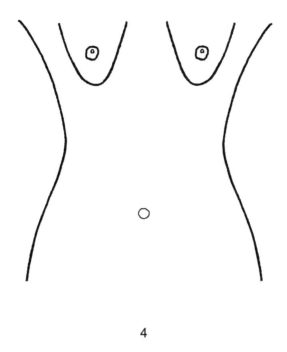

4

Shape 4: "The pagoda." A sharp breast, whose nipple is pointed upward. Such women are often very athletic and have a strong sexual appetite. Problems are more a challenge than a burden for them. They are proud when they do not have to ask for anything. At times they are also vain, while at the same time being extremely sensitive. Their relationship to their own children is too superficial at times. They see only black or white in love: they are either very giving to a partner, or despise him for a lifetime.

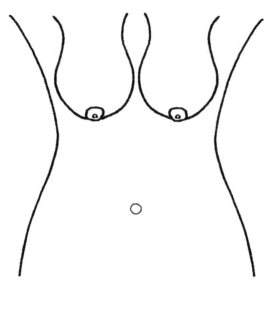

5

Shape 5: "The papayas." The breasts are full and heavy so that they sag downward. Here, too, the teachings Body Feng Shui say that these women will often give birth to very healthy children. They are also among the best homemakers and mothers. They can endure difficult circumstances without complaining. If the body of such a woman is very round at the same time, then this also predicts a happy life, including old age.

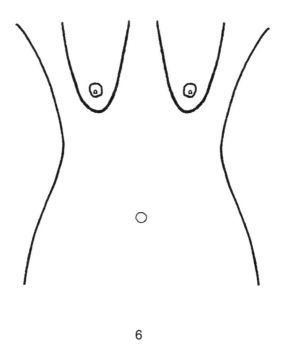

6

Shape 6: "The bamboo scales." Same as shape 4, but sagging a bit more. Women with such breasts have more health troubles than others, and do not expect luxuries from life. They are full of understanding and are very forgiving. Even if they have a lot of children, none of them will be neglected.

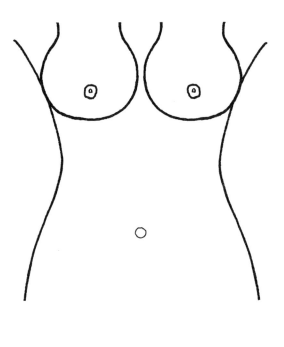

7

Shape 7: "The temple bells." A large, full shape, which is pointed slightly downward. Women with such breasts have strong maternal instincts, which on occasion extend even to the partner. Such women are very tender and soft and respect social order. They complete their daily tasks to perfection. They will not seduce, but rather wait to be conquered; they are also very sentimental. These women usually do not have to worry about money.

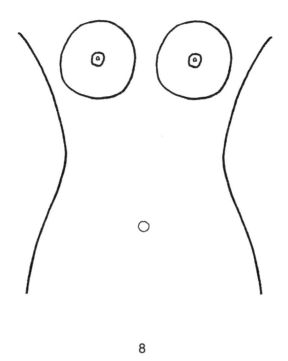

8

Shape 8: "The honey melons." A perfectly round shape. This is often regarded as the most beautiful female breast shape, even though the personalities of women with such breasts often exhibit rather male characteristics. Such women get along with everybody, are very charming, and are also very flexible. They enjoy life past the kitchen and enjoy loving and being loved.

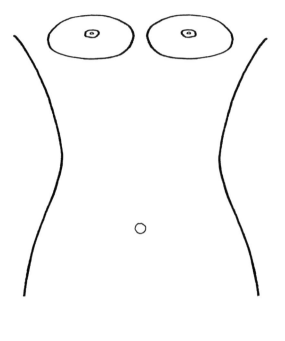

9

Shape 9: "The mangos." An oval shape that rises only slightly from the rib cage, with the lower part being more fleshy than the upper, which gives the impression of the nipples being erect. The personality of these women is often more male; they are self-confident and occasionally rude. They have a very balanced financial sense: there is neither too little nor too much. These women enjoy solitude and rarely have maternal instincts. Their love life takes place more in the imagination than in reality. They are very focused in all their endeavors, which is why they usually enjoy successful careers.

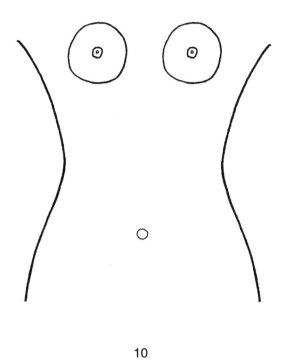

10

Shape 10: "The mandarins." A shape similar to the honey melon, although it appears to be much smaller. Women with such breasts have an exciting love life and reach their long-term goals because of their patience. They like to completely own their partners, which often prompts them to give up a lot for this specific goal. Money, on the other hand, is never safe with them.

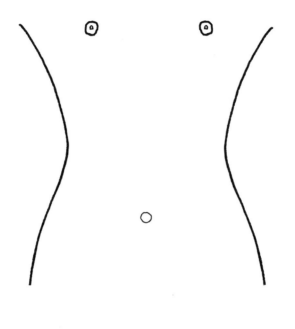

11

Shape 11: "The coins." A very flat shape with a very small hill. Women with this build often unite two contrary characteristics within themselves: on the one hand they act like a mature male, on the other like a little girl. They have varied taste in love matters. These women clearly show what they like and dislike. Long-term thinking is foreign to them, and they like to act as if they were dependent. They always need external aid to reach success.

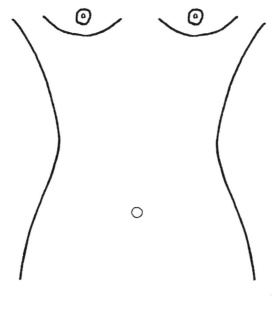

12

Shape 12: "The flower bud." This shape resembles a flat curve, the breast of a girl at the beginning of puberty. Women with such breasts have a very balanced character, even though their physical condition is rather weak. They often set goals that are too high for themselves. They do not act very maturely in love matters.

再生花

FIGURE 51. Tsai Shann Hua, The Petals of Reincarnation

The Jade Gate: "The Perfection of Woman's Being"

An ancient Chinese proverb that is over a thousand years old says, "Internal beauty is much more important than external beauty." And another, much older says, "A man should choose a woman for her moral values, not for her beauty." In modern Chinese, the words for "internal beauty" and "moral values" sound almost like slang for what literature so nicely refers to as the "jade gate."* The task that men have here is not an easy one; after all, neither "internal beauty" nor "moral values" nor the "jade gate" are visible at first sight. So how can a man make the right decision? Here too the teachings of Body Feng Shui can help. The first suggestion is to draw an analogy between visible and covered lips. If the lips of the mouth are full and open, the same is true farther below at the jade gate. The analogy works similarly for small, long, thin lips. Another way to obtain information by external physical appearances lies in the nose. If the sides of the nose are well formed and strong, the same will apply to the muscular abilities of the vagina, which always corresponds to the nose. The depth of the vagina is in direct correlation to the valley between the upper lip and the nose (figure 45, letter *A,* on page 127); the longer this valley is, the deeper the vagina.

Even though the jade gate is of some importance in one's love life, it does not guarantee eternal happiness. A comparison can be made here: There is no such thing as a completely perfect Feng Shui house; that is why it is important to find out who belongs in which house. Only then does a Feng Shui house become perfect. If we apply this thought to a relationship and one's love life, then we will realize that there is no such thing as the perfect partner. That is why it is important to find out who works well with whom. Of course, it is much more difficult to judge a person than a house, especially because people are constantly changing and developing. That is why nobody should expect to find a perfect relationship from the start. Here, too, a reciprocal and neverending development is necessary. One can compare this process to gardening: it is good to fertilize flowers, trees, and lawns, but it is not always essential, in contrast to watering, which is always essential, but where the right amount has to be considered in order to avoid causing damage.

---

*A literary term for the vagina.

FIGURE 52. Nin Wei Nu Tsen, The Perfection of Woman's Being

With this in mind, what does it mean to be a perfect woman, and how can that state be reached? Nobody is perfect by themselves, but only through others. That is why it is so important to be able to recognize the right partner. Body Feng Shui was developed specifically for this purpose. It helps one avoid mistakes and find happiness in life; the energy of life in the jade gate is the lock.

The Jade Stalk: "The Perfection of Man's Being"

The only female Chinese emperor, the famous "Lady Wu," felt obliged to stick to the traditions of her predecessors. These emperors had up to 3,000 concubines, who lived in the palace as "side-women." Naturally, the empress did not want to break with this tradition, and so instead of side-women, she had "side-men." It is also said of Lady Wu that she knew all the secrets of how to enjoy a man. Moreover, she developed a system according to which she chose her men: They had to have fair skin (the ancient Chinese beauty ideal), a fine face, and a large, strong body. The empress even developed a theory on how to find the right "jade stalk"* and did not hesitate to teach her theory to her daughters and some of her female confidantes, so that they would be able to choose the right men for her. Those men who passed the test were allowed to move into the palace and to meet the empress. Her theory went as follows:

The tip of the jade stalk should resemble a freshly opened litchi fruit. The stalk itself should have the strength of young bamboo, and its energy should be such that it could be used when necessary, but that it was quiet when there was no need for it. The shape and behavior of the jade stalk could furthermore be derived from the nose, for which the following applied: If the sides of the nose are well defined, then this will be mirrored in the tip of the stalk, whose form is always the same as the nose (see the section on the nose).

---

*A literary term for the penis.

In patriarchal China it is said that "man resembles a teapot, woman a teacup." According to this, a pot could have numerous cups, while the converse was not possible (with the exception of Empress Wu).

For the Body Feng Shui philosophy neither the behavior of the empress nor the patriarchal saying is of value, since in this teaching only mutual complements are important, and the question is how to find the best complement so that a perfect unit can arise. Just as for a woman's being, in order to find happiness in life a man finds perfection in the right partner. The energy of life of the jade stalk is the key.

FIGURE 53. Nin Wei Nan Tsen, The Perfection of Man's Being

The Ten Most Important Points on the Face

It is said that "in each man's face his story is written." That this is no exaggeration should have become obvious after reading this chapter on the "Laws of Harmony." By way of conclusion, I want to sum up what has been said in order to show that the most important points of life can all be found in the face. At the same time their significance will be explained as well (see figure 54).

Point A stands for all movements a person makes in his or her life (travels, moves, changes of workplace). If this shape is positive, it means that all movements will be positive. But how does one recognize a positive shape? These points should be clearly visible, no hair should be growing on them, and the area should be mostly smooth. Moreover, it is important that the *chi* color also be positive (see the section on "Chi in Human Beings").

Point B represents fame. This point is positive if there is neither hair growing nor slight hills. Here, too, a good *chi* color is necessary.

Point C (the eyebrow) relates to social relationships. These are good if the eyebrow has a positive shape (see the section on eyebrows).

Point D tells of health. This point should be free of hair and be neither too far from nor too close to the eyebrows. In this case the point will be positive and the health good.

Point E stands for marriage. This point has to be flat, free of hair, and free of marks—then it is positive and marital life will be good.

Point F relates to the estate. There should be enough space between the eyebrow and the eye, the bone above it should not be noticeable, and the skin should be taut. If these conditions are met, material wealth will be positive.

Point G stands for love and relationships and is between the eye and the cheekbone. If it is not visible, it is positive, which will have good effects on relationships.

Point H gives information about the happiness and personality of the person. This point is positive if it is higher than the cheeks and is without ups or downs; it should also not be too pointed. If

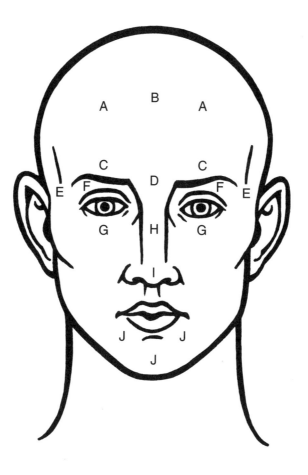

FIGURE 54. The Ten Most Important Points on the Face

all of this is the case, this is a person with a good personality who will find happiness in life.

Point I relates to wealth. It is advantageous if this spot is fleshy and well formed. The skin should be mostly clear, and the chi color good. Under these conditions it is possible that someone could decisively improve her financial circumstances.

Point J stands for life expectancy. It will be positively influenced if this part of the chin is not too pointed and is barely visible.

Now that you have understood the laws of harmony, it should not be difficult for you to recognize the right partner for a happy life. Naturally, self-discovery is a part of this, but practicing that should not be hard for you now either.

自知之明

FIGURE 55. Tse Tsche Tscho Min, The Wisdom to Know Oneself

The Secret of Untarnished Beauty

When I was a little girl, I took every compliment that was given to me as something that related only to beauty. Later in life, I thought only what I liked was beautiful, and disregarded the opinions of others. Even later, I understood that true beauty is a compromise between subjective and objective points of view.

Of course beauty is under the influence of time; it is dependent on where you are, on the circumstances of life, even on religious and political ideals. To give only one example: In Asia white skin is considered especially beautiful, whereas in Europe one should be tan. Two hundred years ago, however, the ideal of white skin reigned in Europe as well, which led to such exaggerated actions as men applying white makeup to their faces. And, because of global cultural exchange, today in Asia the view is slowly forming that a "healthy" brown skin color is at least as beautiful as paleness.

In regard to body measurements and proportions, at least in Asia, Europe, and North America, the ideals seem to be similar; because even though there are very few Asian women that have the desired measurements of 36–24–36, there is still the same ideal regarding well-proportioned and well-shaped body parts.

The same applies to the nose, the European version of which is more highly regarded in Asia than the Asian version, but which is not very important in Europe. In contrast, almond-shaped eyes are very attractive to mostly non-Asian males.

Asians themselves, on the other hand, like the European eye shape, and some have even undergone plastic surgery to achieve this ideal.

Globalization seems to cause a dissatisfaction with what we were given by nature, and leads to the search for the fulfillment of beauty ideals in other cultures. This is understandable when one considers that individual beauty wishes, which consider only outside beauty, are also an international standard. How else could one explain that all of a sudden all women want to look like model X or all men like movie star Y? The beauty industry that is developing from these desires helps only the producers, not the consumers. But are there international laws of beauty? Yes, but they are not natural ones; rather, they are ideals that have been created by those who are always more fascinated by what others have than by what they have (and who, of course, like to profit from this fascination, especially since there are enough victims in the world for this sort of enterprise).

Nonetheless there is an insoluble contradiction in all this: while these man-made laws exist, there also exist the potential buyers, who can only be partially seduced. There always remain enough people who do not care about trends and fads and live their own, unique beauty.

This unique beauty is not a perfect one in the sense of the international fashion community, but a natural one in which there are positive and negative things, as is described in the teachings of Body Feng Shui. The idea is to care for the positive things and to turn negative things into something unique (for example, baldness; one should not be ashamed of it and wear a hairpiece, but rather stylize it into a trademark, which by the way—because of a hormonal excess—also indicates a good libido).

The world is beautiful because of its infinite possibilities and not because of some ominous perfection.

Confucius said, "When you enter a room that always smells evenly of orchids, you will one day no longer be able to realize this pleasant smell. The same goes for muck heaps."

When one gets used to beauty and does not strive to find out whether good things are hidden in it, one will not enjoy it for long. But when one tries to discover what is hidden behind ugliness, one may find an invisible beauty, which surpasses the visible. This is also described by two poems from the Tang Period. The first says:

So beautiful is the sunset,
How sad that night follows.

And the second:

The more clouds there are in the sky,
the more spectacular will be the sunset.

Therefore, trust what you were given by nature. Pay attention to the clouds in the sky, and you will experience a wonderful sunset.

FIGURE 56. Tschien Tschong Fong Chin, Thousandfold Happiness

Physiognomy as the Key to the Soul

As we have discovered so far, Body Feng Shui is a very good instrument for finding the right partner for life. The precondition for applying the teachings is always the careful study of external appearances. This may sound superficial, but over the course of this book, it should have become obvious that there is an internal complement behind each physical characteristic, which is why physiognomy is basically a study of thought. It is the key to the soul of the partner. "Trained" specialists can thus recognize at first glance with whom they are dealing. It would certainly make sense to have the teaching of complements be part of the high school curriculum, so that interpersonal problems and tragedies could be avoided in the future. One example of this is in the arena of love relationships: If both partners had knowledge of Body Feng Shui, divorce lawyers would probably have to look for new jobs, because men and women could learn in their early years who complements them, and who does not. Of course, needs and preferences change over time, but here too Body Feng Shui would help in avoiding mistakes, since one has consciously picked out the right partner. Animals can make this selection based on their sense of smell, which in human beings, unfortunately, has suffered very much through our evolutionary history, and which is why very complicated studies are necessary today to prevent harm and increase happiness. Just as one can realize through psychoanalysis why one appears one way and not otherwise, one can reach the same goal using the inverse method, which is much more pleasant and less harmful.

FIGURE 57. Tschon Shin, The Way Inside

The Secret of the Body

In Western art the naked female body symbolizes perfection, beauty, and harmony. In Chinese painting, however, it is largely ignored. In the West the naked female body can be shown publicly and can be depicted as a symbol for victory, freedom, or peace. This would be unthinkable in Chinese culture; it would be ridiculed and considered rude. Of course this does not mean that the Chinese do not appreciate the female body; rather, it is a self-imposed moral value that prohibits its depiction in public. From these moral values different fashion ideas have also evolved. European fashion emphasizes body curves in an erotic manner and it is very revealing, while Chinese fashion prevents this emphasis. At the same time, however, it encourages the imagination of the viewer, because the secret of the body is not revealed, which may be more erotic than the simple showing of bare skin. That is why in China the erotic is depicted using comparisons to nature. Shoulders turn into soft movements of the willow tree, eyebrows into the shapes of the moon, gazes into autumn lakes, hips into a branching tree, teeth into pomegranates, eyes into almonds, and fingers into bamboo shoots. It is up to the viewer to decode the secret of nature. This method has the advantage that no woman has to be ashamed of her body; on the contrary, regardless of whether it is beautiful or ugly, big or small, it is always the object of poetic imagination, which is more honoring than being merely the object of fleshly desire.

The question remains, however, why it was in China that women were willing to bind their feet because men considered this to be especially erotic. The same goes for the Victorian period in Europe, when women tied their waists so tightly that they resembled a wasp. In both cases women let themselves be turned into accessories for men and destroyed their bodies without rebelling. Why? Because they thought that they would become more attractive to men this way. In the wasp-waist the attraction was in the breasts being pushed forward, while the bound feet pushed the behind backward, so that these sexual body parts were especially pronounced. One should not think, however, that these methods are a thing of the past; they have their place in the present as well, and are only called something different today: Wonder Bra and high heels. Sociologists think that with emancipation the patriarchal era is over. In that case one must ask whether the development of the Wonder Bra and high heels is not a method for men to get back into power. Or are women themselves so blind that they continue to want to be slaves of their own beauty? Everything that exists is beautiful. Spring is beautiful. Summer is beautiful. Fall is beautiful. Winter is beautiful. All the more beautiful, the better one knows the secret. . . .

In Harmony with Oneself and Others

An employee of the emperor's court in China one day went to a monk to ask him for advice. He said, "Look at me, I am ugly and nobody wants to look at me. Nobody likes me, nobody pays me the attention I deserve, nobody follows my orders, but everybody laughs at me. This hurts me, especially because everybody lies to me and cheats me. What should I do?" To which the monk replied, "Be patient! Bear it, suffer through it, let them make fun of you. Stay away from these people, and practice being patient. Do not listen and do not respond, but be patient and wait to see what happens."

The philosophy of patience is regarded more highly in the East than in the West. "A step backward is a step ahead" is the motto of the Chinese view of life, and the basis for Chinese society. Body Feng Shui is also influenced by the philosophy of patience, especially the part that strives for overall harmony. This means that those who do not have positive characteristics should not be unhappy about this, but rather practice being patient, until they have gotten used to their flaws and can start building a harmonious, unclouded relationship with themselves again. It is only in this way that it will be possible to create the sort of harmony that is necessary for friendly interactions with others.

FIGURE 58. Wu Shen Fei Wuo Io, My Body Is Not My Body

Chinese fatalism finds its origins here: one knows where the suffering is coming from, accepts it, and then regains one's balance.

Thus Body Feng Shui is a valuable philosophy that has made it possible to create what is still needed in this world: harmony, out of which peace will arise. At the same time the principal goal is oriented toward the real world, as will be shown in the next chapter.

FIGURE 59. Tschon, Patience

The Message of the Teaching of Correspondences

In chapter one, the sections entitled "The Body and the Five Elements" and "The Right Partner" explained how to find out to which element one belongs. For the choice of people with whom one will have to deal with often or constantly, this knowledge is vital to establishing a positive relationship. The following tables show where harmonies arise and where disharmonies have to be expected. First, however, the character of each element according to the seasons is described:

WOOD

Spring:	cold and thus needs warmth;
	wet, yet thirsty for water;
	budding, but not ready for cutting;
	weak, and thus not requiring a lot of earth.
Summer:	hot and thus thirsty;
	glowing and easily inflammable;
	full of energy but not ready for cutting;
	strong, but not looking for earth.
Fall:	dry and still thirsty;
	old and longing to be cut;
	nippy and looking for warmth;
	cold and looking for the protection of earth.
Winter:	shaking and avoiding water;
	frozen and hoping for warmth;
	shuddering and waiting for earth.

WOOD POSITIVE	FRIENDS AND COLLEAGUES	COUPLES	CHILDREN	PARENTS
Spring	water fire	fire	fire water	fire water
Summer	water	water	water	water
Fall	water metal earth	fire metal	water earth metal	water earth metal
Winter	earth fire	earth fire	earth fire	earth fire

WOOD NEGATIVE	FRIENDS AND COLLEAGUES	COUPLES	CHILDREN	PARENTS
Spring	earth metal	earth metal	earth metal	earth metal
Summer	metal fire earth	metal fire earth	metal fire earth	metal fire earth
Fall	wood	wood water	wood	wood
Winter	water wood	water wood	water wood	water wood

FIGURE 60. Tschien, The Strength of Wood

熊

FIGURE 61. Shon, The Power of Fire

FIRE

Spring: looking for warmth;
wanting wood;
avoiding water;
fleeing the earth;
avoiding metal.

Summer: avoiding warmth;
searching for water;
avoiding earth;
fleeing metal.

Fall: begging the wood;
wanting heat;
fleeing earth;
avoiding water.

Winter: searching for heat;
wanting wood;
avoiding water;
fleeing earth.

FIRE POSITIVE	FRIENDS AND COLLEAGUES	COUPLES	CHILDREN	PARENTS
Spring	wood fire	wood fire	wood fire	wood fire
Summer	water	water	water	water
Fall	wood metal fire	wood fire	wood metal fire	wood metal fire
Winter	wood metal fire	wood fire	wood fire	wood fire

FIRE NEGATIVE	FRIENDS AND COLLEAGUES	COUPLES	CHILDREN	PARENTS
Spring	earth water metal	earth water metal	earth water metal	earth water metal
Summer	wood earth fire metal	wood earth fire metal	wood earth fire metal	wood earth fire metal
Fall	water earth	water earth	water earth	water earth
Winter	water earth	water earth	water earth	water earth

EARTH

Spring: cold and looking for warmth;
weak and avoiding wood;
cool and fleeing water;
weak and looking for more earth;
fearing the wood and wanting metal.

Summer: dry and begging for water;
hot and avoiding fire;
warm and rejecting wood.

Fall: without energy and asking for warmth;
weak and looking for earth;
not thirsty and avoiding water;
avoiding water and thus metal too.

Winter: cold and wishing for warmth;
wet and fearing the water;
fearing the water and thus metal too;
weak and thus not needing wood.

EARTH POSITIVE	FRIENDS AND COLLEAGUES	COUPLES	CHILDREN	PARENTS
Spring	fire metal earth	fire earth	fire metal earth	fire metal earth
Summer	water earth	water	water earth	water earth
Fall	wood earth	fire earth	fire earth	fire earth
Winter	fire earth	fire earth	fire earth	fire earth

EARTH NEGATIVE	FRIENDS AND COLLEAGUES	COUPLES	CHILDREN	PARENTS
Spring	wood water	wood water	wood water	wood water
Summer	wood fire	wood fire	wood fire	wood fire
Fall	metal wood fire	metal wood fire	metal wood fire	metal wood fire
Winter	metal wood water	metal wood water	metal wood water	metal wood water

FIGURE 62. Jang, The Strength of Earth

FIGURE 63. Guei, The Worth of Metal

METAL

Spring: needs warmth;
searches for earth;
fears water;
appreciates wood
and metal.

Summer: needs water;
searches for metal;
wants more earth;
fears wood
and fire too.

Fall: searches for fire;
ignores earth;
likes water;
has no need for wood
or for metal.

Winter: loves the fire;
fears the water;
appreciates earth;
has no need for metal
or for wood.

METAL POSITIVE	FRIENDS AND COLLEAGUES	COUPLES	CHILDREN	PARENTS
Spring	fire	fire	fire	fire
	earth	earth	earth	earth
	wood	wood	wood	wood
	metal	metal	metal	metal
Summer	water	water	water	water
	metal	metal	metal	metal
	earth	earth	earth	earth
Fall	fire	fire	fire	fire
	water	water	water	water
	earth		earth	earth
Winter	fire	fire	fire	fire
	earth	earth	earth	earth

METAL NEGATIVE	FRIENDS AND COLLEAGUES	COUPLES	CHILDREN	PARENTS
Spring	water	water	water	water
Summer	fire	fire	fire	fire
	wood	wood	wood	wood
Fall	wood	wood	wood	wood
	metal	metal	metal	metal
Winter	wood	wood	wood	wood
	metal	metal	metal	metal
	water	water	water	water

WATER

Spring: wet and thus avoiding water;
full of strength and therefore fleeing earth;
full of energy and thus rejecting metal;
cold and looking for fire
as well as wood.

Summer: dry and yearning for water;
weak and asking for metal;
hot and avoiding fire;
dry and not needing wood;
lacking energy and fearing earth.

Fall: pure and yearning for metal;
clear and avoiding earth;
full of strength and desiring fire;
full of energy and thus appreciating wood;
too full and thus fearing water.

Winter: cold and afraid of earth;
freezing and demanding fire;
nippy and wishing for wood;
weak and rejecting metal;
frozen and thus avoiding water.

WATER POSITIVE	FRIENDS AND COLLEAGUES	COUPLES	CHILDREN	PARENTS
Spring	fire wood	fire wood	fire wood	fire wood
Summer	water metal	water metal	water metal	water metal
Fall	metal fire wood	metal wood	metal fire wood	metal fire wood
Winter	fire wood	fire wood	fire wood	fire wood

WATER NEGATIVE	FRIENDS AND COLLEAGUES	COUPLES	CHILDREN	PARENTS
Spring	water earth metal	water earth metal	water earth metal	water earth metal
Summer	fire wood earth	fire wood earth	fire wood earth	fire wood earth
Fall	earth water	earth water	earth water	earth water
Winter	earth metal water	earth metal water	earth metal water	earth metal water

FIGURE 64. Tschuen, The Art of Water

If, during the course of your exploration of the different correspondences, you encounter problematic constellations, do not be worried by that, especially if it is in regard to your partner, your children, or your parents. The result of your exploration does not mean that you now have to leave behind your loved ones, or that you have to see them with different eyes, but rather it means that through Body Feng Shui you have come far enough to deal with *possible* complications early on. Since the knowledge of the five elements refers only to specific characteristics, negative characteristics should be patiently accepted when they occur, and positive ones should be encouraged.

FIGURE 65. Sho Tao, To Go the Right Way

Body Feng Shui in Daily Life

Feng Shui is the ancient Chinese teaching of how one can live healthily and happily in harmony with nature. This teaching refers exclusively to the art of the correct interior and exterior decoration of the home and workplace in order to avoid illnesses and unhappiness and to encourage success.

Body Feng Shui, on the other hand, refers exclusively to the external characteristics of the human body, but its goal is the same.

In comparing these two teachings, one will find that the body resembles the house (the exterior), and the character the furnishings (the interior). If the internal appearance of the house can be improved by certain techniques, the same also has to apply to the body. Most people think that external appearances can be changed only through plastic surgery. In extreme cases, this procedure is necessary and justified. Wise people, however, know that the appearance of a person can also be improved by a change of the internal appearance, that is, the personality. This can be checked using fasting or meditation. Not only the internal appearance but also real physical characteristics can thus be changed.

知命樂天

FIGURE 66. Che Ming Lo Tien, Knowledge Brings Happiness

Have you ever considered why the clothing of people you meet is usually nicer than what you are wearing? And have you ever considered why the people you meet are usually nicer than your own internal appearance?

Body Feng Shui teaches an eternal law: The external appearance reflects the internal appearance and vice versa.

So if you want to have a beautiful external appearance, but do not take care of your internal beauty, both will disappear one day. But if you have internal beauty and take care of it, you will one day have external beauty as well, even if you do not have it right now.

FIGURE 67. Lian Shin, The Internal House

4 Opinions of Chinese Experts

Hsiao Kan Che, a famous Body Feng Shui expert of ancient times, was convinced that all the problems human beings have with one another arise from the fact that people do not look at one another carefully. He also knew, however, that the teaching of correspondences could not stand by itself, and is only effective once it is embedded in a philosophical system that provides guidance for a happy and successful life.

The sage Men Tse, a great Confucian thinker, also knew that a fulfilling life can only be led if it is led in harmony with others; but these others have to be selected carefully to ensure that one can work with them without problems, and to accomplish this the teaching of correspondences is important. Only then can one enjoy the four great parts of happiness: healthy parents, successful siblings, children who are eager to learn, and considerate friends. Of course one cannot choose one's parents or siblings, but one can choose friends and the partner with whom one will have children. And here, too, it is necessary to integrate this happiness into a larger system that will ensure a happy and successful life. This larger system consists of eleven directions, which are represented in the following symbols.

FIGURE 68. Gien Che Fu, Saving Brings Property

FIGURE 69. Chin Che Guei, Hard Work Brings Wealth

FIGURE 70. Hsou Che Sho, Moderation Brings a Long Life

FIGURE 71. Ien Che Tse, Challenge Leads to Obedient Children

FIGURE 72. Gie Che Gien, Pureness Leads to Health

規
致
和

FIGURE 73. Gue Che Ho, The Right Measure Brings Harmony

良致安

FIGURE 74. Liang Che An, Diligence Leads to a Good Conscience

FIGURE 75. Chon Che Chin, Correctness Brings Innocence

FIGURE 76. Inn Che Ging, Being Reclusive Leads to Internal Calm

朗致樂

Figure 77. Lang Che Lo, Proper Thinking Brings Happiness

智知彼福祿壽喜

Figure 78. Che Gi Che Bi Fu Lu Sho Shi, Recognize
in Order to Be Happy